TWO ZULU POETS:
MAZISI KUNENE & B.W.VILAKAZI

Compiled/Edited BY DIKE OKORO

I

TWO ZULU POETS: MAZISI KUNENE AND BENEDICT WALLET VILAKAZI.

Publisher's information, address:
Cissus World Press, P.O.Box 240865, Milwaukee, WI 53224
WWW.Cissusworldpress.com

First published in the U.S.A by Cissus World Press

Cover Design/Photo: Dike Okoro
First Published 2015

ISBN 978-0-967951195

Cissus World Press books are published by Dike Okoro, Founding Publisher.

To the memory of
    Mbulelo Vizikhungo Mzamane
    Obi Wali
    DO Fagunwa

TWO ZULU POETS:

MAZISI KUNENE & BENEDICT WALLET VILAKAZI

Edited by
Dike Okoro

With an Afterword by Lupenga Mphande

CWP
Cissus World Press
Milwaukeee, WI

Acknowledgements:

Mazisi Kunene's poems Published by Permission of the Mazisi Kunene family/Mazisi Kunene Foundation; Benedict Wallet Vilakazi's poems Published by Permission of the Vilakazi family/Professor Herbert Vilakazi.

POEMS OF PROFESSOR MAZISI KAMDABULI WEKUNENE (Extracted from the book entitled, "Indida Yamancasakazi" (The Riddle of The Young Maidens) published by Reach Out Publishers, Pietermaritzburg, South Africa.)

FOREWORD

This comparative anthology of modern and traditional poetry is dynamic in the history of the African people and more particularly the Zulu people whose work is compared. The Kingdom of the Zulu people, history, tradition and culture is associated with the famous King Shaka Zulu who brought the whole nation together. Isizulu poetry is a late comer in the whole literary work of the world. Thus it is important for the pioneers like Professor Bhambada Wallet Vilakazi who wrote his poetry in Isizulu to be acknowledged. Isizulu poetry was recited and there were no records in published books for so many years. The minds of the decades was therefore marginalized and kept under the blanket. It is about time that our heroes are brought into spotlight, their wisdom be heard by many for both social and intellectual consumption.

The idea for capturing these poems came about through a visit by one of the sons of Africa living in America, Professor Dike Okoro who visited the University of Kwazulu-Natal. The idea was then carried by myself, Professor Sihawukele Ngubane to one of the legends of Africa, Professor Mazisi kaMdabuli Kunene who lived over thirty years in the United States of America in exile and continued his inspiration and wrote his poetry in many tongues. Professor Mazisi Kunene, now of the blessed memory, is retired scholar of the University of Kwazulu-Natal who wrote his mind vividly. In this anthology, he writes about freedom, Americans living in the United States who want to come back to Africa, Children of Africa in America, Whites and other racial groups living in South Africa during Apartheid era, African wisdom, Zulu history and its people like Nandi, the mother of King Shaka the Great. Professor Kunene shares his experience in exile through poetry and he has never stopped writing.

Professor B.W. Vilakazi in his poems showcases the traditional poetry written in Isizulu. The poems in this anthology touch on Zulu

VI

history, belief systems, traditions, arts and culture. They are also cultural statements that encourage African people, including those in the Diaspora, to stand up for their identity.

It is a great pleasure to be part of this historic anthology whose voice is about to be heard all over the world. I do hope this anthology will carry the message of our African poets through the minds and continue to inspire more souls and individuals. The poems assembled here were translated for the convenience of those who do not understand the language of the Zulu Kingdom. Having the collection of poems available in both English and Isizulu will assist the reader to read Isizulu with understanding.

Professor Sihawukele Ngubane, PhD (Natal)
Head, School of Undergraduate Studies
Faculty of Human Sciences
University of Kwazulu-Natal, Durban

INTRODUCTION

As a poet and a scholar, once I came across the English translations of Zulu poetry by Mazisi Kunene and Benedict Wallet Vilakazi, I felt a sense of admiration for their courage but also of compulsion to expose a representative selection of their works in both English and isiZulu for the public to read. For five decades one of the subjects of this book, Mazisi kaMdabuli Raymond Kunene, dazzled minds in Africa and beyond with his efficacious poems and essays written first in isiZulu and then translated into English by himself. An impressionable bard of the highest order, his poems are a meeting ground for stories celebrating the human condition, life in Africa and how in Africa modern times is influenced by ancestral ties, and the modern world of postcolonial Africa. These poems are as much a fecund window to Africa for readers familiar with his writing and those reading it for the first time to experience the vision, visionary commitment, and creative hindsight of a poet whose opus helped in transforming African literature in indigenous languages and African poetry in English laced with orature.

Kunene holds the distinction of being the first and only African poet to be honoured by UNESCO as poet laureate of Africa and Arab nations, a global recognition he humbly accepted and would later state, during an interview with Reddy Vasu titled "The Writer as Philosopher: An Interview with Mazisi Kunene," that being a "poet laureate just means that I'm one of the best poets. I am not-what is the word-different about that. I am definitely-there is no doubt about that-one of the very best that Africa has produced in a long time." Kunene's modesty on display here is certainly not an aberration. Great artists have been known to shy away from self-promotion. Instead I feel the phrase "I'm one of the best poets," as he puts it, says it all. And, based on his literary output, originality of thought, and steadfast devotion to writing poetry rich in the

Zulu cultural matrix and African cosmology, he was far ahead of his peers and was clearly one of the greatest African poets of the twentieth century. In a moving tribute to Kunene that appears in UMAFRIKA, South African fiction writer and professor of English, Mbulelo Mzamane declares:

Mazisi Kunene's artistic and political peers Alex
La Guma and Keorapetse Kgositsile,
characterise the symbiotic relationship between
revolutionary poetry and liberation politics
as follows: The poet articulates the dreams of
a people for a better life, the liberation movement
fights to make the dreams a reality. Although
it is impossible to put a simple caption, circumscribe
or contain his work in a condensed milk tin,
Mazisi Kunene located himself within this tradition.
It is pertinent, therefore, to reflect on his contribution
to the unfolding culture of liberation in South Africa.

Kunene's poems, written in isizulu and translated into English, illustrate his commitment to writing in his indigenous language, a trend that has for almost five decades been in practice among African and world writers pushing for the recognition of indigenous literature. As a notable voice associated with the epic poetry tradition, Kunene's poems focus on themes and folkloric elements that at once inform readers on the importance of the oral tradition to his poetic imagination. This aspect of his writing has been lauded by numerous scholars and contemporaries. For instance, Wole Soyinka's declaration in the essay "Cross Currents: the new African after Cultural Encounters" reminds us of the necessity of oral tradition as a viable resource that empowers the contemporary artist, stressing the need for the contemporary artist to "imaginatively transform those elements that render a society unique in its own being, with potential for its progressive social transformation" [Soyinka: 1982: 52].

Soyinka's avowal lends validation to the importance of this book. Aside from being a friend of Mazisi Kunene, I have followed and studied his poetry for years. I also admire his political commitment to the African National Congress (ANC) as its Director of Finance in 1972. During his time in office Kunene helped in organizing the historic South African Exhibition Appeal, an anti-Apartheid event that drew the support of illustrious artists such as Pablo Picasso, Marc Chagall, Giacometti, Ben Enwonwu, Robert Rauschenberg, and Henry Moore. In fact, his commitment as an artist was inseparable from his love for the liberation of his South African homeland. It is the same love I find in his passionate poems that convey narratives enriched with Zulu tales and universal themes. Kunene drew his inspiration for poetry from his Zulu heritage. This is a fact that has been referenced by numerous scholars. Pitika Ntuli and Johannes A. Smith, in the essay "Speaking truth to Power," described Mazisi Kunene as a visionary poet and summarized their declaration by citing Sandile C. Ndaba's argument that Kunene's visionary commitment entails the utilization of resources from the Zulu cultural matrix and Zulu oral tradition. And that furthermore his poetry draws on Zulu cultural references and allusions while at the same time impacting on cultural issues.

I want to add that the idea for this book arose from Kunene himself tasking me to go ahead with the adoption and completion of the project. To him I owe whatever success comes out of this publication. I had read his work extensively in graduate school and had travelled to South Africa, Durban, to be specific, to visit him at his home. Two hours spent interviewing and chatting with him about literature, African writers, his own writing, Western canon, and the role of the writer in society, left me with a plethora of ideas to put into practice. We couldn't carry on with our interview because Kunene was unwell at the time and had been in and out of hospital. I promised to be back after he encouraged me to visit again before my departure for the United States and I left on that occasion.

But we would not meet again before my return to Chicago in June of 2003. I returned to my home in the United States armed with the resources I needed to complete this book. Prior to my trip, I had no knowledge of the kind of material I expected to dabble onto. Zulu literature in translation had offered me so little to learn from and educate myself on the foundations, transformations, and eventual modernization of the literature itself. For the record, I have to be careful with my diction, especially the word "modernization". Writers are not averse to change. This one can easily discern from Africa's contact with Europe as well as Europe's contact with other indigenous peoples of the world, with emphasis on the Maoris of New Zealand, Native Americans and the Pacific Islands community. That contact, whether good or bad, has been largely responsible for the resistance movements experienced today in the literatures of indigenous peoples across the world. And the same can be said in terms of Kunene's poetry. It opens new doors as much as it challenges the reader to think, maximize his or her judgment on its veracity, and assume a position of neutrality based on pure appreciation of poetry at its finest.

In Kunene's work one is bound to find some of the finest poems composed. His poems, though enriched with Zulu oral tradition and African cosmology in particular, explore the social context in which the writer finds himself in a South African world still confronting the parameters posed by an intolerable Apartheid system that negated the values of Bantu education and the role of the writer in society. Kunene wrote his poems, one may say, from his passion and deep love for Africa, Zulu culture, society, and culture and his homeland of South Africa. Despite living in the United States for three decades, he never wavered in the issues he confronted or explored creatively in his poems. His past and future were always major subjects he grappled with in his poems and essays. For the outsider, unfamiliar with his poetry, there is bound to be the lack of interest shown toward his topicality, which centred on nation-building and ancestral praises. But even then, Kunene's poetic output symbolized much more than these aspects of his writing. Kunene wrote poetry that explored the oral traditions and literary history of Southern Africa. In his poetry one finds the frequent representation of dramatic episodes that celebrate the cultural life of his people. Also, nature and the natural world are used in his poems as mirrors revealing to us the way human actions today are inseparable from the natural order of things. It is this aspect of his writing that I find to be worthy of exploration. In fact, a quick glimpse of his volumes of poetry, beginning with Zulu Poems and ending with echoes from the mountains, which I compiled and edited, illustrate the very best of Kunene's poetry. His poems, aside from his epics that are long, are typically short, imagistic, and thought provoking narratives. Sometimes while reading his work I'm drawn to, or shall I say reminded of, making comparisons to the poetry of Benedict Wallet Vilakazi, better known as B.W. Vilakazi, whom Kunene himself told me represented in his poetry the intricate nuances that the ancestors had meant for us to celebrate.

Vilakazi remains a pivotal name when South African literary history is discussed at length. His scholarly contributions to Zulu literature and South African literature in the indigenous languages represent one of the most fascinating events in the history of South Africa. The South African scholar Ntongela Masilela reflects on Vilakazi's place in South African literary history, citing the distinguished South African intellectual of the New African Movement, H.I.E Dhlomo, as he states:

Approximately three years earlier Dhlomo wrote a poem in which he placed Vilakazi in a context of traditional poetry from antiquity to the modern times, because the Zulu poets' linguistic innovations had not been discernable and had not been accorded the acclamation they deserved. Celebrating Vilakazi as a poet of rare genius, Dhlomo wrote that he had brought something new and strong into Zulu language as well as into South African culture (p.71)

This is arguably a worthy assessment of Vilakazi's importance, for the hallmark of his art was to use literature that addressed the landscape and realities of his South African homeland to examine the human experience. These are some of the engaging aspects of his poems in this book that sustain and preserve his genius as an important voice for his generation.
I think this is what Masilela attempts to share with readers in his book, The Cultural Modernity of H.I.E. Dhlomo, where he contends:

Indeed, Benedict Vilakazi's name has remained sacred In South Arican intellectual and cultural history. Dhlomo marvelled at the unity of the critical and the poetic in Vilakazi's intellectual imagination. In Africa too he has been celebrated by Ngugi wa Thiong'o. In an essay celebrating the release of Nelson Mandela from a 27-year imprisonment in 1990, Ngugi invoked the name Vilakazi among other South African writers as exemplifying the best in South Africa that is essential to the whole of the African continent.

The above quote shows clearly one of the reasons why Vilakazi merits mention among the literary giants that Africa has produced. His place in Africa's literary history is secured, and this book supports the initiative to bring to students and scholars across the world some of the finest poems representing the creative imagination of

XIII

B.W. Vilakazi.

Vilakazi's poetry shares with readers his love for the natural world of his South African homeland, his closeness to his family, and the deep views he held concerning the role of blacks in South Africa. Conversely, Kunene's poems separate him from Vilakazi in many ways. Kunene, I must say, is as relevant to modern African literature as Geoffrey Chaucer, William Shakespeare, and Sophocles are relevant to the canon of Western Literature. His poems in this book share with readers his view of history as a foundational basis for comprehending the history of the black family in the West, and his acknowledgment of pan-Africanism as a vehicle for African diasporic solidarity. In the poem "Africa's People In America," his speaker uses the first person "I" to negotiate meaning and reflect on the black experience in America, while also revealing the excitement at finding the bond that exists between Africans on the continent and Africans in the Diaspora, using Shaka's lineage in Zulu mythology to clarify the peculiar links that establish the importance of pan-Africanism:

I have seen our people
Who were enslaved in many countries
Who were enslaved and taken overseas, the place of the dogs
They are beautiful like images of ancestors
They are beautiful like black grinding stones.

I have found them when I was still amazed
I have found them when they had soft eyes
Being heroes of the water world
Indeed it is the one that is long, it is the one that begets
It is the one that covers them, with the rays of the sun.

I am with them and embrace them

Cooling down their wounds and those that are white
Showing them trails including Africa
I am not alone I am with the ancestor of King Shaka
I am with many ancestors who caused them to cross the ocean.

The allusion to ancestors, according to the social realm described by Kunene here, represents a solidarity of Africans in the Diaspora. Kunene takes a historical stance in his assessment of their progression and existence as a people who still bear the identity of their heritage. This is the point he highlights as he states: "I have seen our people /Who were enslaved in many countries / Who were enslaved and taken overseas / the place of the dogs / They are beautiful like images of ancestors." The idealistic approach of the speaker in this poem is guided by the confession of the traveller. This same confession can be looked at as the testimony of the exiled voice. After all, Kunene lived in the US for thirty-six years. His reference to the ancestors here is influenced by the Zulu belief in the significance of the ancestors in our lives. Kunene therefore remembers the customs of his people and uses its model which is grounded in communal prosperity to appreciate the thriving models of the African family in the Diaspora. There is a direct reference to the slave trade and its ramifications in this poem. But the reference bears no bitterness. Instead hope and joy are what the reader takes away from the poem. And Kunene rightfully concludes his message with hope, stating: "I am with them and embrace them /Cooling down their wounds and those that are white / Showing them trails including Africa / I am not alone I am with the ancestor of King Shaka / I am with many ancestors who caused them to cross the ocean." There is also an implied lesson in this poem. Kunene is hopeful of teaching the dominant culture how to embrace the residues of the post slavery era as a part of their own history, the human history, without failing in acknowledging that doing so will benefit the representative communities of the enslaved and the slave owner.

In yet another poem titled "In America—I Remember Afrika" Kunene's speaker laments in a sort of way that resembles an epiphany, using the exile voice to reflect on the exile's circumstances while reinforcing the spirit of memory and the celebration of his heritage:

In this day I hear the call of Africa
When I look at the world of strangers
I see shadows, I see mountains
I see the sun, I see people like this and that
I hear a dog barking yonder
I hear people laughing in the plain
Even the ants that follow each other have paths
They bring me songs, they bring me news
They bring me poems of my ancestors.

Unlike Kunene, Vilakazi's poems use a direct sarcasm to poke fun at the transitions taking place in postcolonial Africa. A poem that hinges on this aspect of Vilakazi's preoccupation is "What is Knowledge?" where he looks at the educational system and uses rhetorical questions to express his concerns:

Tell me friend!
What is knowledge?
I dress up nicely,
I carry a cane,
I get on the road,
I eat well?

Tell me my peer!
What is knowledge?
Is it going to school?

XVI

Reading the book,
Until I am bald,
Turning over pages?
Tell me mother!
What is knowledge?
Is it to be a speaker?
Be applauded by the whole world,
Interpreting the laws,
Without understanding?

The theme of modernity is also expressed in Vilakazi's poetry. Here he is sceptical of education, asking "Tell me friend! / What is knowledge? / Is it going to school? / Reading the book / Until I am bald?" He finds the acquisition of knowledge taking place in school very uninspiring and untrustworthy. Thus, he concludes that there is grave danger in the model copy-cat syndrome which involves Africans taking after ideas and ways foreign with little room for intellectual creativity and originality. This conclusion is grounded in the very foundation of the philosophical question Vilakazi poses in the poem "Higher Education."

Unlike the poem "What is Knowledge?" Vilakazi makes a sudden shift in "In the valley of a thousand hills (KWADEDANGEND-LALE),"choosing to dwell on the landscape and explore his appreciation of nature. In this poem the natural world of his South African homeland is painted in a way that gives the reader a vivid image of the poet's homeland, particularly Durban as in this case:

I remember home, far away
Where the sun rises
Above high mountains,
It sets red below
Until darkness comes

And the peaceful silence,
When you get outside to smell,
You smell with your nose
You shroud the whole body
With the moistening sea breeze.

I also remember the Qwabe clan
In the land of the umkhambathi trees
That is full of wasps and thorns,
Where we put
Temporal shelters
Surrounded by mountains
With cliffs and rocks
Covered with algae
Green like the hair
Of a sheep that is newly born.

Here Vilakazi dwells largely on the physical topography of his homeland. Like Kunene, Vilakazi delves into the intricate lives of the characters of the histories. He describes passionately his deep love for the place of his birth. In this poem the poet's philosophical and emotional sides elevate the experience captured. In addition, the poet's sense of identity is alive as he describes the KwaZulu-Natal landscape and ecological features, especially the fauna and flora, of his homeland. Also the use of proper nouns in making direct allusions to places and personal names provides for the reader the poet's strong affinity with the landscape, geographical locations, and ancestral iconography that link him to the land.

In fact, the aforementioned poem by Vilakazi brings to mind C.L.S. Nyembezi's declaration concerning Vilakazi that, "he [Vilakazi] was gravely concerned lest the Zulu heritage be lost to the younger generations. In his poems he refers over and over again to the need for preserving those things which are sacred and precious to the Zulu nation" (1973: xix).

On a personal note, this work will leave a lasting impression on the minds of those familiar with the poetry of Mazisi Kunene and B.W. Vilakazi for several reasons. The relevance of both writers to the evolution of modern African literature is incontestable. Like their contemporaries from the continent, they have, by virtue of their literary production, served as flag-bearers for the continent. Their works speak to this declaration. I owe much of my success to many people, including Professors Sihawukele Ngubane, formerly Head of the African Languages Department at the University of KwaZulu-Natal, Durban, South Africa and Professor Ntongela Masilela, in whom Kunene found a true friend, brother, protégé and scholarly comrade. My friendship with Masilela lit up when I first met Kunene and it has remained solid ever since. It was Masilela who called me on that fateful evening in August of 2006, while I was taking my evening walk down the road to relay the news of Kunene's passing. The shocking occurrence left us chatting for long over the telephone but did not deter my aspiration to see to the completion of this project.

It is my hope that this book, a bilingual anthology of poetry by Mazisi Kunene and Benedict Wallet Vilakazi, will help revive interest in indigenous African poetry in translation among students and faculty. I close this introduction with the words of Chinua Achebe, who when pressed to opine on the relevance of his attempts at invoking incidents in his novel Anthills of the Savannah had this to say about Mazisi Kunene's poetry to his interviewer, Jane Wilkinson, in Africa America Asia Australia (Rome) vi, (1988) : "as Africans today, we should make it a habit of invoking these powerful images from our history, legend and art...you don't have to repeat everything that Kunene has said, but just mention the keyword, the password, and the whole image is called up in the imagination of those who know, who are aware, who are literature in our traditions. I think this is very important."

Dike Okoro, PhD
Northwestern University
Evanston, USA

Works Cited
Masilela, Ntongela. The Cultural Modernity of H.I.E. Dhlomo. Trenton: AWP 2007, 69-70.

Mzamane, Mbulelo. Mazisi Kunene-imbongi yesizwe.
    UMAFRIKA. August 25-31, 2006.
    http://www.cas.org.za/projects/images/mazisi6.pdf
Ndaba, Sandile. "Visionary Commitment in Mazisi Kunene's Ancestors and the Sacred Mountains." Retrieved 6 October 2013. http:singh.reshma.tripod.com/alternation/alternation6_1/05SND-ABA.htm

Ntuli, Pitika and Johannes A. Smith. "Speaking truth to Power." Alternation6 (1). p1-20.

Schulte, Rainer & John Biguenet (eds). 1992. Theories of Translation. An Anthology of Essays from Dryden to Derrida. Chicago & London: University of Chicago Press.

Soyinka, Wole. "Cross Currents: The African after New Cultural

Encounters." In Armithanayagam, G (Ed). Writers in East-West Encounter. (London: Heinemann, 1982)

Thengani H. Ngwenya "B.W. Vilakazi: The Poet as Inspired Prophet." Alternation Journal. Retrieved 02 September 2013.www.alternation.ukzn.ac.za/doc/05.

Vasu, Reddy. "The Writer as Philosopher: Interview with Mazisi Kunene." South African Journal of African Languages. Nov 96, Vol.16 Issue 4, p 141.

Wilkinson, Janet. "Interview with Chinua Achebe." Africa America Asia Australia (Rome), 4 (1988): 69-82.

CONTENTS

PART I

MAZISI KUNENE

- POEMS in ENGLISH and ZULU -

FREEDOM

We shall be your followers even long after you are gone.
We will search for that promised stone,
We will take the marriage where it began,
Saying it is the one that made us to persevere
Even when we will hear your voice.
It will be far, becoming faint with the wind.
We believe that you will return because you belong to us.
We are brave even when you ostracize us.
We see you from the inner side of your eye
We say remember, we are your intermediaries.
We say we brought him, our brother, bearing him on our shoulder.
We say he was about to place the stone
With which we shall remember you for your sacrifice.

INKULULEKO

Siyoba umbelebele nasemuva kwakho
Silifune lelo litshe lesethembiso
Siwuthathe umendo lapho uqala khona
Sithi yiwo lona osusenze sabekezela
Sathi nokuba silizwa ilizwi lakho
Selikude, seliyakunyamalala nemimoya
Sathi yiya uyakubuya, ungowakithi
Siqungq isibindi nokuba ususiphika
Sikubuka phakathi emehlweni akho
Sithi: Khumbula phela yithi abashumayeli bakho
Yithi size naye umnewethu simetshethe ngehlombe
Yithi ebesiyakulibek' ilitshe
Ngalo sithi sesiyakukhumbula owakho umnikelo.

THE HELPER BECOMES THE VICTIM

You neglected me ever since I healed you.
I remember the one who gave birth to me,
Who said, "The helper becomes the victim."
She did not mean just you, but the whole world.
By the way, what wrong did we do to the people of Europe
For them to bear us such grudge?
By the way, it is us who found them roaming around.
We gave them land and they turned against us with guns.
Here they are, swaggering as if they were of substance,
As if we don't know yet we know that the wealthy ones were left at
home.

UMLUNGISI UZITHELA ISISILA

Awusanginaki wena selokhu ngakwelaphayo
Sengikhumbula yena ongizalayo
Yena owathi "umlungisi uzithela isisila:
Wayengasho wena wayesho umhlaba
Kakade sasibenzeni abantwana baseYurophu
Baze basibekele amagqubu angakaya?
Ingani yithi esabathola belalatheka
Sabapha ilizwe basiphendukela ngezibhamu
Yibo laba asebeqholosha ongathi bebesutha
Ongathi abazi siyazi abasuthayo basel'emuva emakubo.

AFRICA DURING TIMES OF TRIBULATIONS

They have abandoned you, your loved ones,
They have run away because you are a disgrace.
They have rejected you even in the ears of the nations
Preferring to praise those moving towards assimilation,
Speaking in languages that you don't know
So that you do not understand.
But I whom you did not choose
I have knelt before the homesteads.
I say, although you have avoided me I will follow you.
You will fill up the yards with your fields
So that those who deserted their homes will return.
I will plead with them in a soft language
Until they see, until they become enlightened,
Until they praise you together with us in ceremonies.
Even I who is unwanted I will be there,
I shall be there eternally; I shall be there always.
Not with my eyes closed with love of blindness,
But seeing at the depth, where you will shine.

I-AFRIKA NGEZIMINI EZINZIMA

Sezikulahlile izithandwa zakho
Sezikubalekela ngokuba uhlambazekile wena
Sezikuphika nasezindlebeni zezizwe
Ziqoka izibongo zabasekuthathekeni
Zikhuluma ngezilimi ongazaziyo wena
Zithi wukuba ungayukuzwa
Kepha mina obungangikhethanga
Sengiguqe ngamadolo phambi kwemizi
Ngithi, nokuba ugengelezile ngiyakukulandela
Uyakuwagcwalisa amagceke ngezinsimu zakho
Nabo ababhungukileyo bayakubuya.
Ngiyakubancenga ngolimi oluthambileyo
Baze babone, baze bahlakaniphe,
Baze bakubabaze nathi emikhosini.
Ke mina ebenginyamanambana ngiyobengikhona
Ngikhona ungunaphakade ngikhona enjalweni
Ngingavalekanga amehlo ngothando lobumpumputhe
Kepha ngibona emajukujukwini lapho uyakube umuhle wena.

TO MY SISTER SITHANDIWE

Oh sister, and mother, I thank you
I am thankful for your multitudes of hearts
I am thankful for your tender hands
They are the ones that fed the provider
They nurtured him even when he was grown up
They told stories until he fell asleep
When they saw him wake up they brought him water
They brought milk from the cows
It was the one that nurtured the hearts
They say the depth that we had moulded
Up to now we stand at the gate with our hand stretched
Asking for the name that he gave to you.

KUDADEWETHU USITHANDIWE

O dade, Nomame, ngibonga wena
Ngibonga izinhliziyo zakho ezimakhulukhulu
Ngibonga izandla zakho ezithambileyo
Yizona zimondlileyo umondli
Ziye zamcathamisa umuntu esekhulile
Zamxoxisa izindaba waze wozela.
Zathi ukumbona esephaphama zaletha amanzi
Zaletha ubisi lezinzwakazi,
Yilo lunonophalisa izinhliziyo
Zabona kude emajukujukwini osulubumbileyo
Nakalokhu simi emasangweni sikhangezile
Sicela igama yena akunike lona.

THOSE NATIONS

Those clever nations
That discard female and male elders at ancestry homes
They are the nations with no humanity.
They are the ones that wither like leaves
And are blighted by strange diseases.
When they wake up in the morning they rub a wasted face
Hoping to rejuvenate it with cosmetics, and the face is gone.
They are shocked by wrinkles that should be there,
Yet the rivers of a person's richness dwell within.
They are the ones that deepen the roots of mind
They are the ones that fulfil a person's joy
They are the ones that will overflow even in the eyes of happiness.

LEZO ZIZWE

Lezo zizwe ezihlakaniphileyo
Ezilahla izalukazi namaxhegu emazaleni
Yizo zingenabuntu bomuntu
Yizo ziyakugongobala njengamahlamvu
Zize zivuthulwe nayizo izifo ezingaziwayo
Kube kuyasa zihlikihla ubuso obekade baphela
Zibufuna ubusha nangemigcobo yamakha, sebadlula
Ziyayethuka imibimbi obekuyiyo ifaneleyo
Kanti imifula yokunona komuntu iphakathi
Yiyo ijulayo nasezimpandeni zengqondo
Yiyo isiyakumnandisa umuntu
Yiyo iyawuphuphuma nasemehlweni entokozo.

WHEN YOU RETURNED WASTED

It wasn't going to be like this if you had listened to me,
If you had planted a plot below my homestead,
If you had drunk with me from cold fountains,
If you had entertained me in the afternoon with folktales,
If you had stayed with us with my children's laughter,
If you had merrily partaken roasted meat with us,
If you had drunk from the calabash of my grandfather,
If you had joined to pay respects with us to his izidlodlo,
If you had bowed before the mountain of Mandiki!
But you couldn't be disciplined; you were out of control
You had eaten the sacrifices of the ancestors of foreign nations.

*izidlodlo: feathers stuck on a man's cultural head-ring to symbolize status in society

MHLA USUBUYA USUSHAYEKILE

Kwakungayuba nje ukuba walalela mina
Ukuba watshala isiza enzansi komuzi wami
Ukuba waphuza nami emithonjeni ebandayo
Ukuba wangihambela ntambama nangezinganekwane
Ukuba wahlala nathi nohleko lwabantabami
Ukuba wayitshefuza nathi inyama yokosa
Ukuba waphuza okhambeni lukababamkhulu
Ukuba wahlonipha nathi izidlodlo zakhe
Ukuba wayikhothamela intaba yaMandiki
Kepha wawungasakhuzwa wawusudlebelekile
Wawusudle imihlabelo yamaThongo ezizwe.

IN THE CALABASHES OF NATIONS

I wish that by the end of this day
I should have drunk from many calabashes.
Those from China and from Arabia and from Malaysia;
Those from India and from Mongolia and from America;
Those from Europe and from Russia and from the Maori
And from all the enlightened nations of the world.
But at the end I go back to my roots,
I return to those from Mbokodweni, the tasty ones
Of the largest historic fountains
Which are the inherited treasures hidden from us.
We will drink repeatedly until we reach the end!

EZINKAMBENI ZOLWAZI LWEZIZWE

Ongathi lungathi luphela lolu suku
Ngibe sengiphuzile ezinkambeni eziningining
NezaseChayina nezase-Arabia nezaseMaija
NezaseNdiya nezaseMongoliya nezaseMelika
NezaseYurophu nezaseRashiya nezaseMaori
Nazo zonke zemihlaba ngemihlaba ehlakaniphileyo
Kepha ekugcineni ngibuyele kwezakithi
Ngibuyele kuzo zaseMbokodweni ezimnandiyo
Ezimithombokazi ibomvu ngokuvuthwa ndulweni
Yizo zona zingamafa afihlelwe thina
Sesiyakuwaphinda size sifike ekugcineni.

NANDI OF BHEBHE

You mother, you have walked a long way
You were not scared with your children
Please protect our daughters
They are the main hope of our land
(However, a big tree does not wait for rain)
Please strengthen the eyes that are strained
Because the women are the ones endowed with vision
They see things at the depth
They who don't display their worthiness with muscles
They who write when they want or keep quiet
With you who provide us with a broad back
We nurture the generation of generations
So that they will venture where you have walked
They will mould a big calabash
So as to quench the thirst of all African nations.

UNANDI KABHEBHE

Wena mame unhlanhlathe izindlela
Wena ungesabanga lutho nabantabakho
Akewusingathe nazi izintombi zakithi
Yizo ziyesethembiso esikhulu somhlaba wethu
(kube umuthi omkhulu kawulindi-zimvula)
wena kawuqinise amehlo asegcwele ubuthakathaka
ke lokhu yiso isimame sethu sona sihlakaniphile
sona sibona kude emajukujukwini
sona singagabe ngazikhwepha ezimsiphasipha
sona sibhalayo uma sithanda sona sithulayo
ke ngawe wena osenzele umhlane obanzi
sesikhulisa zona izizukulwane zezizukulwane
zona ziyawuhamba lapho uhambe khona
zona ziyawubumba ukhamba olukhulu
zizeziphuzise zonke izizwe zama-Afrika.

WHITE PEOPLE

As white people being red
They chose a colour; they chose white.
Yet what is of the whole world is of the sun.
They have deceived themselves, they deceived one another.
They say the bowl they eat from is forever
Because they are children born yesterday.
It is the dangerous weapon they carry that is frightening.
It frightens cowards until they cower,
Until they agree mentally with their deceit.
But in fact they are also scared!
They know they are like this because of the fairy tales
They tell the nations.

ABELUNGU

Abelungu njengoba bebomvu nje
Bazikhethela umbala bazikhethele okumhlophe
Kanti kona kungokwezwe lonke kungokwelanga
Bona bazikhohlisile, bakhohlisana
Bathi lesi sitsha abadla kuso yiphakade
Kanti kungoba bengabantwana bezelwe izolo
Yiso isikhali esibi abasiphetheyo esethusayo
Sethusa amagwala aze agongobale
Aze avume nangenqondo inkohliso yabo
Kanti empeleni kwabona yimihla sebesovalweni
Bezazi banjenjenje yingenxa yezinganekwane abazitshele izizwe.

AFRICA'S PEOPLE IN AMERICA

I have seen our people
Who were enslaved in many countries,
Who were enslaved and taken overseas, the place of the dogs.
They are beautiful like images of ancestors;
They are beautiful like black grinding stones.

I have found them when I was still amazed;
I have found them when they had soft eyes,
Being heroes of the water world.
Indeed it is the one that is long, it is the one that begets
It is the one that covers them with the rays of the sun.

I am with them and embrace them,
Cooling down their wounds and those that are white
Showing them trails including Africa.
I am not alone! I am with the ancestor of King Shaka,
I am with many ancestors who caused them to cross the ocean.

I was there when Solezwe was born.
I saw him with my own eyes when he crawled,
I saw him with my own eyes when his legs got strong,
I saw him with my own eyes when he walked top,
I heard his voice when he was praising.

There is a big mountain
Where we will all meet,
Where we will dance until sunrise,
Where we will cast the memory stone
And say: "Our history is wide like those who are forever."

ABANTWANA BASE-AFRIKA ABASEMELIKA

Sengibabonile abantwana bethu
Ababethunjiweyo amazwe ngamazwe
Ababethunjiweyo bayiswa phesheya kwelezinja
Bahle banjengemigido yamaDlozi
Bahle banjengezimbokodwe ezimnyama.

Ngibafumene mina ngisamangele
Ngibafumene besenamehlo athambileyo
Beseligagu lomhlaba wamanzi
Ingani yiwo omude, yiwo ozalayo
Yiwo ubafukamele nangemisebe yelanga.

Sengihambisana nabo ngibanga
Ngibapholisa izilonda nezimhlophe
Ngibakhombisa imikhondo neyase-Afrika
Angingedwa ngineDlozi likaShaka
NginamaDlozi amaningi ayebawelisa.

Ngibe ngikhona lapho kuzalwayo uSolezwe
Ngimbone ngamehlo esegaqa ngamadolo
Ngimbone ngamehlo eseqina imilenze
Ngimbone ngamehlo esehambela phezulu
Ngiwezwile amazwi akhe esebongelela.

Kukhona intaba enkulu
Lapho siyawuhlanganela khona
Lapho siyawugida khona kuze kuphume ilanga
Lapho siyawubeka ilitshe lesivivane
Sith: "Imilando yethu ibanzi izingangeyamaphakade".

21

IN AMERICA – I REMEMBER AFRIKA

In this day I hear the call of Africa!
When I look at the world of strangers
I see shadows, I see mountains
I see the sun, I see people going here and there.
I hear a dog barking yonder,
I hear people laughing in the plain.
Even the ants that follow each other have path.
They bring me songs, they bring me news
They bring me poems of my ancestors.

EMELIKA NGIKHUMBULA I-AFRIKA

Kule mini ngizwa imbizo ye-Afrika
Ngibe ngiyabheke emhlabeni wamankengane
Ngibon' izithunzi ngibon' izintaba
Ngibon' amalanga ngibon' abantu benjeyaya
Ngizwa nenja ikhonkotha emaphesheya
Ngizwa abantu behleka emathafeni
Namatsheketshe lawa alandelanayo anem'mibondo
Angilethele izingoma, angilethele izindaba
Angilethele izinkondlo zawobabamkhulu.

TO LAMAKHOSI, THE THANKED ONE

Well my daughter, now more beautiful even in the mind,
The one that shines like the sun;
You have received a beautifully decorated calabash.
You now have to present it to the crowd
So that when they see it, they will know that you are born of the
Kunene.
The ones who are generous, the ones who are doubly intelligent.
The one for the men, the one for the women.
You will now even carry on your back the disabled
So that when they reach the destination they will sing that hymn,
Saying the world is wide because of the people.
They won't be referring to people on two legs,
But to those who started the essence of humanity.
The one that germinates, the one that ripens
The one that attracts even the passer-by!
Yes, so that they do not forget others who are still waiting on earth
Saying there is a place where people are beautiful
When they sit down and tell the stories of that place.

KU LAMAKHOSI EBONGIWE

Ke ntombi yami usumuhle nangengqondo
Yona ibalelayo njengamalanga
Usulutholile ukhamba oluhle olufekethisiweyo
Usuyakulubeka phambi kwezixuku
Zithi zingalubona besezazi uzalwa eKunene
Bona bephanayo bona bebuhlakani bukabili
Obunye ngobendoda obunye ngobomfazi
Usuyakuzibeletha nezinkubela
Zize zithi zingafika ekugcineni zilihube lelo hubo
Zithi: Umhlaba wande kangaka ngabantu
Zingasho laba abahamba ngezinyawo
Zisho bona abaqale ubuntu bomuntu
Bona buhlumayo bona buvuthwayo
Bona bubiza nabo abahamba ngendlela
Yebo bazebangakhohlwa abanye balindile umhlaba
Bathi: Kukhona indawo lapho abantu bebahle
Lapho behlala phansi baxoxe izindaba zakhona.

Part II

BENEDICT WALLET VILAKAZI

- POEMS in ENGLISH and ZULU -

WHAT IS KNOWLEDGE?

Tell me friend,
What is knowledge?
I dress up nicely,
I carry a cane,
I get on the road,
I eat well?

Tell me my peer,
What is knowledge?
Is it going to school,
Reading the book
Until I am bald,
Turning over pages?

Tell me mother,
What is knowledge?
Is it to be a speaker,
Be applauded by the whole world,
Interpreting the laws
Without understanding?

Tell my father,
What is knowledge?
Come my boy,
Let me pull your ears:
"Talk a little
Do bigger."

(B.W. Vilakazi – Amal' eZulu)

YIN' UKWAZI? (WHAT IS KNOWLEDGE?)

Ngitshele mngane!
Kuyin' ukwazi?
Ngigqoke kahle,
Ngiphat' induku,
Ngigcwal' umgwaqo,
Ngidl' ezibomvu?

Ngitshele ntanga!
Kuyin' ukwazi?
Ngukuy' esikoleni,
Ngifundane nencwadi!
Ngize ngiphum' impandla
Ngipheny' amaqabunga?

Ngitshele mame!
Kuyin' ukwazi?
Ngukuba yisikhulumi,
Ngibatshazwe yizwe lonke,
Ngichazane nemithetho
Ngingenal' ulwazi lwayo?

Ngitshele baba
Kuyin' ukwazi?
Woza mfana wami
Ngikudons' indlebe:
"Khuluma kancane
wenze kakhudlwana."

(B.W. Vilakazi - Amal' eZulu)   [Translated by Gabi Mkhize]

28

IN THE VALLEY OF A THOUSAND HILLS

I remember home, far away
Where the sun rises
Above high mountains
It sets red below
Until darkness comes
And the peaceful silence.
When you get outside to smell,
You smell with your nose;
You shroud the whole body
With the moistening sea breeze.

I also remember the Qwabe clan
In the land of the umkhambathi trees
That is full of wasps and thorns,
Where we put
Temporal shelters
Surrounded by mountains
With cliffs and rocks
Covered with algae
Green like the hair
Of a sheep that is newly born.

Where we frolic
Singing like the wind,
Climbing mountains
Meandering along rivers
Flowing downwards.
Where no one returns,
Where the elders say

Is the dark sea
That has been roaring and heaving
Ever since they opened their eyes.

I too, I stood above
I bowed down before Mkhambathini
I looked down below,
I saw the smoke rise
I asked without knowledge.
They whispered in my ear,
They showed me from
The top of Mgungundlovana
Stretching down to Mhlali
And above Mgungundlovu.

I started to be amazed
Seeing dark fields
Producing blossom corn
And ripening sorghum.
The doves and the birds
Singing on tree branches,
Echoing the ripening season.
My eyes were drawn
To the top of the high veld.
I saw them looping the boughs.
Then I saw climbing
Black ladies
Carrying pots,
Balancing them on their heads,
And their bodies glamorous
Because of care,
Seeking the nation's fame.

Behind these ladies
I saw the tails stand erect,
And the shields of young men.

I saw the propping up
Of the ladies and young men.
I saw a lady's man conquering
By giving them gifts of beads.
I stood and fell jealous
I consoled myself on the other side.
When I looked down below
The nearest msengane tree,
I saw beautiful herds
Of goats and sheep.
Among them
I saw shepherds herd them,
Directing them home.
I looked at the Ocean
I was faced with haze,
A cool breeze fanned me,
Blowing through the trees,
I listened and turned around,
Yet it was dusk.

I looked down the river
I saw the water shining,
As if it were brightened.
So was my shadow,
It also reflected inside.
I looked at myself and I was satisfied.
Down at uMlazi and uMkhomazi,
You should visit there

You will see these things.
They will open your heart.

The mkhambathi trees of this place
Even in winter blossom.
Yet when they shed
They have no power to awaken.
Yes, me too, I will blossom;
I will be full of berries,
I will reproduce like palm trees
Covered with fruits
Through the moon of mkhambathi
Down to our nation of KwaZulu.
I will stand upright
Like the mountains
Of KwaDedangendlale.
They have a charm for beauty
That I saw attracting the white man.
He walked; he walked and stopped,
He also parked his car,
He got out and sat down,
He took out his pipe and smoked,
He looked until he cried.

Me too I am like that.
I get drunk on these mountains,
I go astray and get lost,
I get lost in the valleys.
Those that bear flowers
They mix the scents
Of minduze tree and water lilies
That bloom in the pools

That decorate the tranquil water
That calm into a beautiful row.

I got drunk and staggered unsteadily
Until I was overtaken by the mist.
In the middle of the forest
I met with baboons.
They scared me,
They shouted at me,
They were singing the song
That they sing in the evening.
I heard others wake up,
Animals and birds.
I saw a nightjar staring at me.
I milked for her children,
I slept under the moon,
I was born on the back by the sand.
The pillow was the grass;
I put my head on branches of grassroots.
I rolled over,
I looked at the stars
Which appear and disappear below,
And the umthala grass turning with the earth.

Give me a place like this,
You, Ancestor of my father,
Where I will attain the strength,
And collect the imagination of the Zulu nation
And encase it in a pot.
I sing the lyrics of the poem
Shaka sang when he conquered
Rejoicing at kwaDedangendlale,

Stumping through Khahlamba mountains,
Triumphing over Langalibalele.

Remind me of the Zulu-ness
That I see at Thukela.
I cross at Ndondakusuka.
While there, I was clad in it,
I strained my eyes across.
Even there I saw the beauty.
I wished I moved aside
And prepared a place to rest
Under the palm and munga tree,
And spoke to the ancestors.

You, ancestor, you are here,
You invite me by the Ntshangwe,
You show me kwaBhota
And the nation of MaQadi.
I saw Mafukuzela;
As he breathed I ate.
When I was full I stayed.
I heard about Dedangendlale
I looked toward the West
I remember home, far away.

(B.W. Vilakazi)

KWADEDANGENDLALE (IN THE VALLEY OF A THOUSAND HILLS)

Ngikhumbule kud' ekhaya
Laph'ilanga liphumela
Phezu kwezintab'ezinde,
Lishone libomv'enzansi
Kuze kusondel'ukuhlwa
Nokuthul'okucwebile,
Laph'uphuma phandl'unuke,
Uhogele ngamakhala,
Uzigqum'umzimba wonke
Ngomoya wolwandl'omanzi.

Ngikhumbule nakwaQwabe
Ezweni lemikhambathi
Elinemivi nameva,
Lapho sigxumeka khona
Amaxhokovan'ezindlu
Sisingethwe yizintaba
Ezinamawa namatshe
Amboze yimbingcizane
Eluhlaz'enjengoboya
Bemvan'esanda kuzalwa.

Lapho sigingqika khona,
Sihuba njengemimoya,
Sikhwelana nemimango
Egamanxwe yimifula
Eholob'ibhek'enzansi
Lapho kungabuywa khona-----

35

Bath'abadal'uma besho
KukwaLulwandl'olumnyama
Olugubhayo luveva
Selokhu bavul'amehlo.

Nami ngimile phezulu.
Ngiqoshem'eMkhambathini
Ngabuka phansi enzansi,
Ngabona kuthunq'intuthu,
Ngabuza ngingenalwazi,
Bangihlebel'endlebeni,
Bangikhombisa kusuka
Phezulu koMgungundlovana
Kudwebe kushon'eMhlali
Nangenhla kwaseMgungundlovu.

Ngaqala ngamangala
Ngibon'amasim'amnyama
Ekhihliz'ikhab'ummbila,
Esevuthiwe,
Amajuba nezintaka
Zitshiloz'emagatsheni
Ziwenanel'ukuvuthwa.
Amehl'am'adonsekela
Phezulu kwezinkangala
Ngibona zikhwel'imingqangu.
Kuzo ngabona kukhwela
Izintoka'ezimnyama
Zithwele amagobongo
Ziwayekelel'ekhanda,
Nemizimb'icwebezela
Ngenxa yokuzicwengela

Zifun'udumo lwesizwe.
Ngemva kwalezi zinkehli
Ngibon'amashob'emile,
Nezihlangu zezinsizwa.

Ngabona nokushelana
Kwezintombi nezinsizwa.
Ngabon'amasok'enqoba,
Ziwakhunga ngobuhlalu.
Ngema ngafikelw'umona,
Ngaziduduza nganxanye.
Lapho ngibheka ngaphansi
Kwemiseng'ebiseduze,
Ngibon'imihlambi emihle
Yezimbuzi neyezimvu.
Phakathi kwayo ngabona
Abelusi beyinqanda,
Beyiqondis'emakhaya.
Ngabheka ngakwaLulwandle,
Ngahlangana nofasimbe,
Ngabethwangumoy'omnandi,
Wez'usondela ngemithi,
Ngalalela ngaguquka,
Kant'ilanga lishonile.

Ngabheka phans'emfuleni,
Ngabon'amanz'esekhanya,
Kwangath'asekhanyisiwe.
Kanjal'isithunzi sami
Naso savela phakathi;
Ngazibuka nganeliswa.
Phans'eMlazi noMkhomazi,

37

Uyovakashela khona
Uzibone lezi zinto.
Ziyokuvul' inhliziyo.

Amanzi ayokukhanya,
Ekhanyisw'izinkanyezi
Zasezulwini emafini.
Um'unenhliziy'egcwele,
Uyohlala phans'ubonge
Amathong'oyihlomkhulu
Akuzalela kwaZulu, KwaBuhlebungayindawo,
KwaMfulisagcwelamanzi,
KwaTshanibuseluhlaza.

Imikhambathi yakhona
Nasebusik'iyathela,
 Kant'imith'iphundlekile,
Kayinamandl'okuvuka.
Yebo, nami ngiyothela
Ngigcwal'amajikijolo,
Ngiyethe njengamasundu
Agcwele'izihlekehleke,
Ngay'inyanga yomkhambathi,
Phansi kwelakithi kwaZulu.

Ngiyokuma ngithi phuhle,
Ngifuzane nezintaba
EzikwaDedangendlale,
Ezinekhambi lobuhle
Engibone lidl'umLungu,
Wahamba wahamba wema,
Wamisa nemoto yakhe,

Waphuma wahlala phansi,
Wakhiph'igudu wabhema,
Wabuka waze wakhala.

Nami kaningi nginjalo,
Ngidakwa yilezi ntaba,
Ngilahleka ngingatholwa,
Ngedukile ngezigodi
Eziqhakaz' izimbali
Zihlanganisil'iphunga
Leminduze namazibu
Aqhakaz'esizibeni,
Ahlobis'amanz'athule
Ecwebe ngohla'oluhle.
Ngidakwe ngaphuphutheka
Ngaze ngaficwa yinkungu.
Ngiphakathi namahlathi
Ngahlangana nezimfene,
Zangethusa zingikhuza.
Ngalalela kud'ongoqo
Benikezelan'igama
Abalicula ngokuhlwa.
Ngezwa kuvuka nezinye
Izilwane nezinyoni.

Ngabon'uzavol" engikha,
Ngasengel'abantabakhe.
Ngalala phansi kwenyanga
Ngibelethwe ngumhlabathi;
Isiphuku kungutshani,
Ngacamel'esiqundwini.
Ngashayana nengqimphothwe

Ngibukel'izinkanyezi
Ziphuma zishon'enzansi,
Nomthal'uguquka nezwe.

Ngiph'indaw'enjengalena
Wena Thongo likababa,
Lapho ngiyokuba namandla,
Ngiqoq'umqondo kaZulu,
Ngiwuvalel'embizeni.
Ngihay'amahub'enkondlo
UShak ayihay'enqoba
Eqa kwaDedangendlale,
Ayagqule ngoKhahlamba,
Adl'uLangalibalele.

Ngikhumbuze ngobuZulu
Engibubona oThukela.
Ngiwel'eNdondakusuka,
Nakhona ngibhince bona.
Ngelul'amehlo phesheya,
Nalapho ngibon'ubuhle.
Sengathi ngabe ngideda,
Ngendlale ngiziphumuze
Phansi kwesundu nomunga,
Ngikhulume namathongo.

Nina mathongo nilapha,
Ningimema ngase Ntshangwe
Ningikhombisa kwaBhota.
Nasezweni lamaQadi
Ngabon'uMafukuzela.
Wath'ephefumula ngadla,

Ngathi ngesuthi ngahlala.
Ngezwa ngoDedangendlale,

Ngaqalaz'eNtshonalanga,
Ngakhumbula kud'ekhaya.

(B.W. Vilakazi) [translated by Gabi Mkhize)

BECAUSE YOU NOW SAY

Because I always smile
I show happiness.
I sing with a voice,
Even though you are in a hollow in the ground
Of the green stones of the earth.
Now you say I am like a pillow
That does not feel any pain.

Because my mouth laughs
And my eyes are lowered,
I bent my knees and bowed down,
And my hair greyed
Full of the load dust.
I held a peak in my hand,
And a shirt without back.
Now you say I am like a rock
That does not know death.

Because every evening
I have taken off the chain
Of the day's hard work,
I meet with my people
And we dance,
We dance to the traditional songs
Invigorating the blood,
Banishing the tiredness.
How, you say, I am an animal
That dies as a new one is born.
(B.W. Vilakazi)

NGOBA …SEWUTHI (BECAUSE YOU NOW SAY)

Ngoba ngimamatheka njalo,
Ngikhombisa nokwenama,
Ngihlabelela ngephimbo,
Nom'ungifak'emgodini
Ngaphansi kwezinganeko
Zamatsh'aluhlaz'omhlaba
Sewuthi nginjengensika
Yon'engezwa nabuhlungu.

Ngob' umlomo wam' uhleka,
Namehl'am'ebheke phansi,
Ngifingqe ngabek'idolo,
Nezinwele sezimpofu
Zigcwel'uthuli lomgwaqo,
Ngipheth'ipiki ngesandla,
Neyemb'elingenamhlane—
Sewuthi nginjengedwala
Lon' elingakwaz'ukufa.

Ngoba njalo ngakusihlwa
Sengikhumula iketango
Lomsebenz'onzim'emini,
Ngihlangana nabakithi
Siyogadlela nendlamu,
Singoma ngamadala
Asikizelis'igazi,
Kuphele nokukhathala ----
Sewuthi ngiyisilwane
Esifa kuzalw' esinye.

(B.W. Vilakazi /Zulu)
[translated by Gabi Mkhize]

43

BECAUSE I AM DULL

I am crashed by ignorance
I don't even understand the laws.
But I hear the smell
And my house I build
Under the cliffs.
The grass is my house,
A sack bag is my cloth.
Now you say I am a mute
I don't even house a tear
That sheds into a heat.
It drops in the good hands
Of the ancestors that see everything.

(B.W. Vilakazi)

NGOBA NGIWUMNGQUPHANE

Ngoba ngiwumngquphane,
Ngibulawa ukungazi,
Ngingaqondi namithetho,
Kodwa ngizwa ingiphanga;
Nendlu yami ngiyibeke
Ngaphansi kweziwa zetshe;
Utshani buyindlu yami,
Isaka liyisivatho-----
Sewuthi ngiyisiduli,
Kanginalo nonyembezi
Olucons'enhlizyweni,
Luwel' ezandleni ezinhle
Zamadloz'abuka konke.

(BW Vilakazi)
[Translated by Gabi Mkhize]

I WILL THEN BELIEVE
(I miss dad. He died in my hands in June 10, 1933 at Mvoti)

I will then believe that you are dead,
If the sound of the birds above
And the night brightly decorated with heaven stars;
Stars of heaven;
If the morning star and other stars
That brighten darkness like the moonlight
Have disappeared eternally.

I will only believe that you are dead
If mountains and rivers that flow,
The North and the South that explode,
If the cold of winter and the dew
That has covered the grass today and yesterday
Have disappeared eternally.

Like the star that is falling from far above,
And the bodies collapsing like wild banana trees
That surround the stones and the sands of the sea,
I saw it like a dream when they covered it,
I waited when it slowly and slowly vanished.

When the stars faded, and you too
I saw you frowning and losing the heroism,
In addition I will never believe
That all my existence is worth nothing.
I will only believe that you are dead,
If the sun and moon are dead

And fall to the ground,
If the earth disappeared eternally.
(B.W. Vilakazi– Inkondlo kaZulu)

SENGIYOKHOLWA-KE (I WILL THEN BELIEVE)
(Ngikhumbula ubaba. Wafela ezandleni zami ngoJune 10, 1933, eMvoti)

Sengiyokholwa ukuthi sewafa –
Um' ukukhala kwezinyoni zaphezulu –
Nobusuku obuqhakaz' izinkanyezi zezulu;
Um' inkwezane yokusa nezinkanyezi –
Ezikhanyis' umnyama njengonyezi-
Sezanyamalal' ungunaphakade.

Sengiyokholwa ukuthi sewafa –
Um' izintaba nemiful' egobhozayo,
Inyakaktho neningizim' evunguzayo;
Um' ungqoqwane wobusika namazolo
Abemboz' utshani namuhla nayizolo –
Sekwanyamalal' ungunaphakade.

Njengenkanyez' edilika phezulu kude,
Nomzimba wawa njengemithi yezigude
Ehenqe ugu nezihlabathi zowlandle,
Ngawubona kuhle kwephupho bewumboza,
Ngawulindela uya ngokuya uphoza.

Ngenkathi kufiphal' izinkanyezi, nawe
Ngabon' unyinyiphala kwaphel' ubuqhawe,
Phezu kwaloko angiyukukholwa neze,
Konke ukubona kwami kulize leze.
Sengiyokholwa ukuthi sewafa,
Uma ilanga nenyanga sekwafa,

Kwawel' enhlabathini yamagade,
Kwashabalala ungunaphakade.

(B.W. Vilakazi - Inkondlo kaZulu)
[translated by Gabi Mkhize]

HIGHER EDUCATION

When I talk nonsense I was thinking
That I would find happiness.
If I finish the book,
I unlock written notes,
Analyzing them I see.
Today I feel the migraine headache.

I have wasted a lot of time
Turning over the leaves
Of the books written by a Whiteman.
I sit alone the whole night
Until just before the sunrise.
Today my eyes are hurting.

I visited black poets
Singing praises of the King's mind,
And some praising the traditional beer in the sacred
of the house.
I picked their wisdom,
I mixed it with that of white men.
Today they are conflicted in my head.

The one who doesn't know everything about these
 things,
And the one who sleeps the whole night
Reading nothing until the dawn,
Avoiding Caesar and Cicero
And Shaka and Ngqika and Mshweshwe.
Today he is happy at heart.

Those we grew up with and didn't study,
I meet them and they look down on me.
When I walk barefoot,
Them, they come in cars;
They blow the dust at me and leave.
Today they are like mushrooms of the earth.

When I try to let go,
Chasing crumbs in the trails
Of my peers who are doing well,
I find myself still tied up
By the sinews of education.
Being myself pressurizes me.

Today I think of the time
When we are old and done;
I search my bags,
I feel the books poking out.
They follow me wherever I go.
Let me see what they say!

I see the names of the whole nation.
The eyes of the ancestors are watching over me;
The ancestors have put the shields.
They are lying under the earth;
They say I must enter so that I partake
In the calabash, because I did not forget.
I partook and I ate and put on the shelves.
I preserved it for the Zulu family
To remain and partake from the books,
To fight each other explaining
The thing that I wrote at night

That I never intend to write.
I was persuaded by you ancestors of the nation,
Confusing the mind at night.
At that time I will be dead.

(B.W. Vilakazi – Amal' eZulu)

IMFUNDO EPHAKEME (HIGHER EDUCATION)

Uma ngibheda ngangicabanga
Ngithi ngiyothol' ukujabula
Uma ngigogodana nencwadi,
Ngiqaq' amafind' abhaliweyo,
Ngiwachaza njengoba ngibona.
Namhla ngizwa kuqaqamb' ikhanda.

Sengachith' isikhath' esiningi
Ngiphendulana namaqabunga
Ezincwad' ezibhalwe ngumLungu,
Ngihlezi ngedwa busuku bonke,
Kuze kucish' ukuphum' ilanga.
Namhla ngiqaqanjelwa ngamehlo.

Ngavakash' izimbong' ezimnyama
Zihay' imiqondo yamakhosi,
Nezinye zibong' utshwal' emsamo.
Ngafak' ukuhlakanipha kwazo,
Ngakudiya nokwezabamhlophe.
Namhla zixaben' ekhanda lami.

Ongaqondi lutho ngalezi zinto,
Nozilalel' ubusuku bonke
Engafundi lutho kuze kuse,
Engama' uSiza noSisero,
noShaka noNgqika noMshweshwe,
namhla' uyathokoza ngenhliziyo.
Esakhula nabo bangafunda,
Ngihlangana nabo bangeyise.

53

Ngithi lapho ngishay' unobhanqa,
Bona baqhamuke ngezimotho,
Bathuquz' uthuli bangishiye.
Namhla banjengamakho' omhlaba.

Ngibe ngisathe nginokuyeka,
Ngixosh' imvuthuluk' esemikhondweni
Yawontagayeth' abami kahle,
Ngifumane ngisakhulekiwe
Yizona zisinga zokufunda.
Ubumina buyangigqilaza.

Namhla ngicabanga ngesikhathi
Lapho sesigugile saphela,
Ngiphuthaz' ezikhwameni zami,
Ngizwa ziqhubushile izincwadi,
Zingilandela noma ngiyaphi.
Ake ngibon' ukuthi zithini!

Ngibon' amagam' esizwe sonke.
Amehl' amadloz' angibhekile;
Amathong' abeke nezihlangu,
Alalele ngaphansi komhlaba,
Athi mangingene ngikhothiswe
Ukhamba ngoba ngingakhohlwanga.
Ngikhothe ngadla ngabek' ethala,
Ngibekel' usapho lwakwaZulu,
Lusale lukhoth' ezincwadini,
Luxabane lodwa luchazana
Nezint' engazibhala ebusuku,
Ngingazange ngizisukele ngibhale,
Ngibeleselwe yinina mathong' ohlanga,

Ningixabanis' ingqond' ebusuku.
Kuleyo nkathi ngiyobe sengafa.

(B.W. Vilakazi - Amal' eZulu)

[Translated by Gabi Mkhize]

NOW I BELIEVE
(Lamentation of my father)

Now I believe that you are dead.
Because even though the sun brightens the earth,
I see in the morning the animals grazing,
Whisking their long hairy tails
That whistle like our cows at Mhlali.
Anyway, I have seen the sun set at noon.

Now I believe that you are dead.
The sun sets at noon at Mandlakayise.
When I tried to plead they took me;
They poured water of tears on me.
I saw him lying before they covered him up
I saw the train coming at noon.

It was the same thing with Nomasoni.
The stars of my eyes shut down;
She got cold and she failed to warm herself.
As for me, I stood and my arms were shivering,
Watching at her face fading away.
And the beauty faded and vanished from my sight.

How can I not believe that you are dead?
If your road is open,
I see all the years of your suffering.
You seemed to have left when the door was open
So that others could leave though they were tired.
Yet they followed you and never returned.
They are not coming back, you of the hero of

Mzwangedwa.
They bid farewell, I stood and they left me by myself.
Others I placed at Gulukudela
Where quiet darkness covers them;
Others I planted them at Mhlatuze
Where they are protected by hen.
Because I hear the bell of angels ringing.
It wakes them up in the morning to rush for prayers.
I see them when the sun is red below;
I see them when it is red on the mountain.

They are red down Mhlatuze.
I saw them shining in oppositions;
I listened to the big well
Where sleep fans my grandfather.
I heard the voice say, "Beat the angel
In winter and in summer so that it cries without
sobbing!"

Indeed I am convinced that you are dead.
Because I see in me the hair thinning on my head,
The hair of youth grey hair covering the head,
Giving me respect and the sign of elder-ness.
The one that I saw in you when you were grey and
 getting tired.
After that you went slowly, fading.
Even I saw you fading slowly.
Today I believe that you are dead.
Because in my sleep I see you.
You come with a calm heart,
You take me across the gates and pools
Of wisdom and the paths of intelligence.

And your walking stick I hear it thudding
In front of my eyes, yet not seeing you.
I am like a blind person with eyes of the body.
Yes, now I believe that you are dead.
You have disappeared forever.

(B.W. Vilakazi – Amal'ezulu)

SENGIYAKHOLWA (NOW I BELIEVE)
(ISIKHALO SIKABABA - A Lamentation of my father)

Sengiyakholwa ukuthi sewafa,
Ngoba noma ilanga liwukhanyis' umhlaba
Ngibon' ekusen' izilwane ziklaba,
Ziziphunga ngamashob' anenhlali,
Emhloph' okwezinkomazi zakith' eMhlali,
Nokho sengike ngabona kuhlw' emini.

Sengiyakholwa ukuthi sewafa,
Kwangihlwel' emini ngoMandlakayise.
Ngabe ngiyathe ngincenga bangiyise,
Bangithela ngamanz' ezinyembezi,
Ngambon' elele bengakamembesi.
Ngalibon' iphupho liz' emini.

NangoNomasomi kwabanjalo.
Izinkanyezi zamehlo zacimeza,
Wabanda wehlulw' ukuzifudumeza.
Mina ngema ngaqhaqhazela izingalo
Ngilunguz' ubuso bakhe buhwelela,
Nobuhle benqaba bangifiphalela.

Ngingekholwe kanjan' ukuthi sewafa
Um' umgwaqo wakho uvulekile,
Ngibon' iminyaka yonk' ubhudulekile?
Wena kungathi wahamba umnyang' uvuliwe
Khon' abanye beyophuma sengathi badiniwe,
Kanti sebelandela wena bengabuyi.
Ababuyi, wena weqhawe laseMzwangedwa.

59

Bavalelisa ngime bangishiye ngedwa.
Abanye ngibabeke kwaGulukudela,
Lapho umnyama uthule ubagubudela;
Abanye ngibatshala eMhlathuzane,
Lapho befukanyelw' izikhukukazana,
Ngoba ngizw' insimbi yengelos' incencethat,
Ibavus' ekuseni beyokhuleka baqenqetha.
Ngibabon' ilanga enzansi libomvu,
Ngababona lisemagqumen' ezibomvu.

Izibomvu enzansi noMhlathuzane
Ngizibonile zikhanya ziphikisana.
Ngalalela phansi komthomb' omkhulu
Lapho kulel' uFrans' ubabamkhulu,
Ngezw' izwi lithi: "Shayan' ingelosi
Ebusika nasehlobo ikhal' ingalingozi!"

Kanjalo sengidelil' ukuthi sewafa,
Ngoba ngibona kimi kuqothuk' ekhanda
Izinwele zobusha, izimvu zingikhanda,
Zinginik' ukuzotha nophawu lobudala
Engalubona kuwe uyimpung' usukhathala.
Emva kwalokho waya ngokuya ushabalala,
Nami ngaya ngikubona kancan' unyamalala.

Namuhla sengiyakholw' ukuthi sewafa,
Ngoba kwaButhongo ngiyakubona
Uza nenhliziy' enokuphola,
Ungiweza ngamasango namazibuko
Obuhlakani nezindlela zenkalipho;
Nodondolo lwakho ngiluzwa lugqula
Phambi kwamehl' ami ngingakuboni.

Nginjengempumputhe ngamehl' omzimba.
Yebo, manje ngiyakholwa sewafa,
Wanyamalal' ungunaphakade.

(B.W. Vilakazi - Amal' eZulu)

[Translated by Gabi Mkhize]

WHERE DID YOU GO?

They deceived me, Mandlakhe.
They said I should stay and wait.
You of Makhwathwa had never
Packed and left. You simply
Disappeared and left everything.
You visited with Nomasomi.

I entered your house at home,
They said you were just here.
I went to Pietermaritzburg (Mgungundlovu)
I found the houses red.
People kept quiet, the houses spoke.
They said: "there, there he is."
I went here and there,
I thought I would see you something
Busy at school, working.
Yet, you wanted Nomasomi.

I entered a classroom at school
Children said: "here is the Teacher!"
Yet, they were referring to a resemblance.
I looked at all corners,
I thought I would see you, Mandlakhe.
I asked from the traditional healers.
They turned and looked at each other
They showered me with tears
They were mourning Nomasomi.
I went outside to search.
I searched for roads of the homestead

I searched Pietermaritzburg,
Its doors and mirrors.
Even Ethekwini (Durban) down
The green waters,
Where you were born.
I searched until the day
Became darker because of the night.
Yet, you were going to take Nomasomi.

I stayed under the palm bushes,
The green that hides the mambas,
Those that eat people and birds.
I directed my eyes to the middle
Of the sea full of waves.
I saw them racing,
I looked at the middle,
I saw far, you were two.
Yet, you were with Nomasomi.

I thought I would see you appearing.
The moon rose, I could see it.
I searched with my eyes, I asked.
It said it never saw you.
I folded my arms I turned back
And the woman carrying firewood
Inside the full moon,
I beckoned her, I asked her.
She turned away in the mist of the moonlight
She quickly went straightforward.
I kept quiet I bowed my head.

All are deceiving me.

Even you, you are deceiving me too.
You surprise me in my sleep,
You visit me in sleep,
You bring Nomasomi
Because you know that here
I am like a prisoner and a fool.
You come back and you play games with me
When I wake up suddenly!
I hold the cold air,
My eyes catch the haze.

You are deceiving me, Mandlakhe.
But where did you get out and go?
My feet are worn out
Walking on the path,
Walking and searching for you.
But where did you go?
So now, why did you take her?
Why did you steal Nomasomi?

(B.W. Vilakazi – Amal'eZulu)

NAYAPHI? (WHERE DID YOU GO?)

Bangikhohlisile Mandlakhe,
Bathi mangihlale ngilinde.
Wena kaMakhwatha awuzange
Ubophe uhambe. Wasuku nje
Wanyamalala washiya konke,
Wavakasha noNomasomi.

Ngingen' endlini yakh' ekhaya,
Bathi kad' ulapha khona manje.
Ngay' eMgungundlovu,
Izindlu ngazifica zibomvu.
Kwathul' abantu kwakhuluma
Zona zithi: "nangu nanguya!"
Ngashona lapha nalaphaya.
Ngathi ngiyokubona khathisimbe
Ulibel' esikolen' usebenza.
Kanti' ufun' uNomasomi.

Ngingen' endlini yesikole
Izingane zathi: "nang' uThisha!"
Kanti zisho ukufana.
Ngaqalaza macala wonke
Ngithi ngizokubona, Mandlakhe.
Ngabuza ezinyangeni,
Zaphenduka zabhekana,
Zangithela ngezinyembezi
Sezililel' uNomasomi.
Ngiphume phandle ngayofuna,
Ngifun' imigwaqo yomuzi,

Ngipheny' uMgungundlovu,
Izicabha nezibuko zawo;
Ngisho neTheku phansi
Emanzini aluhlaza
Lapho wazalwa khona.
Ngifune imini yaze
Yahwaqabala ubusuku.
Kant' uzothath' uNomasomi.

Ngihlale phansi kwemithungulu
Eluhlaz' ecash' izimamba
Ezidl' abantu nezinyoni.
Ngiphons' amehlo phakathi
Olwandl' olumagagasi,
Ngawabona' ejubelana.
Ngagqolozela phakathi,
Ngabona kude nibabili.kanti ninoNomasomi.

Ngangithi ngiyothi ngibona
Wena ubuthi qhamu.
Inyanga iphume ngiyibona,
Ngahlunga ngamehlo ngiyibuza.
Yathi ayizange inibone.
Ngakhwic' imikhono ngabuya.
Nenkosikaz' ethwel' izinkuni
Phakath' endilingeni yenyanga,
Ngayiqhweba ngayibuza.
Yangifulathela othulini lonyezi,
Yabhekuza yaya phambili njalo.
Ngathula ngagebis' ikhanda.

Bonke bayangikhohlisa.

Nawe uqobo uyangikhohlisa.
Uyangizuma ngilele,
Ungivakashele kwaButhongo,
Umlethe uNomasomi,
Ngoba waz' ukuthi lapha
Nginjengesiboshwa nesilima.
Uyabuya laph' udlala nami.
Ngithi ngiyavuka gubhubhu,
Ngibamb' umoya oqandayo,
Amehlo ami abamb' ufasimbe.

Uyangikhohlisa Mandlakhe.
Kodwa waphuma wayaphi?
Sengiqothuk' izinyawo
Ngiqabathek' endleleni,
Ngihambe nginifuna.
Kodwa naya ngaphi?
Pho, manje wamthathelani,
Wamebelani uNomasomi?

(B.W. Vilakazi - Amal' eZulu)
  [Translated by Gabi Mkhize]

WHEN I AM FACED BY DEATH

Bury me under the grass,
Next to the trees of mnyezane,
Where branches will cover me
With lush green leaves.
I will also hear as I lie underground,
The grass on top whispering:
"Sleep my love, sleep and rest."

Bury me on top of the dams,
Where the water is calm and still,
And where the small birds
Singing with their voices
Echo the spring season
And come down to drink cool water
Where the sun is no longer hot.

Let me die on the paths
Of the school pupils,
Since shoulders are overcome
By the heavy burden placed on me.
It is the noise of the children
That comforts the souls
That have slept the sleep of eternity.

Bury me in a place like this,
Where the awls of the tongue
Of the woes will not be found.
The gates separating the world
They wake me up from a beautiful sleep.

If you who reads these numbered lines
Reach me, bury me where
The grass on top will say,
"Sleep my love, sleep and rest."

(B. W. Vilakazi)

MA NGIFICWA UKUFA
(When I am faced by death)

Ngimbeleni ngaphansi kotshani
Duze nezihlahla zomnyezane,
Lapho amagatsh'eyongembesa
Ngamaqabung'agcwel'ubuhlaza.
Ngozwa nami ngilele ngaphansi
Utshani ngaphezulu buhleba:
"Lala sithandwa, lal'uphumule.

"Ngimbeleni phezu kwamadamu"
laph'amanz'ethul'enganyakazi,
nalaph'izinyon'ezincanyana
zihlabelela zisho ngephimbo
zenanel'ukwethwasa kwehlobo,
zehle ziphuz'amanzi'apholile
laph'ilanga lingenakushisa.

Ngiyeke ngifel'ezindleleni
Zabantwan'abafund'isikole
Njengob'amahlomb'esehluleka
Yimithwal'ebengisindwa yiyo.
Iyona misindo yabantwana
Eduduza imiphefumulo
Elel'ukulal'okuphakade.

Ngimbeleni endawen'enjena:
Laph' izinsungulo zezilimi
Zenkathazo zingenakuthola
Sango lokwahlukanis'umhlaba,

70

Zingivus'ebuthongweni obuhle,
Uma wen'ofunda lem migqana
Ungifica, ungimbele lapho
Utshani ngaphezulu buyothi:

"Lala sithandwa, lal'uphumule.
(B.W. Vilakazi);[Translated by Gabi Mkhize]

COURAGE

At the gates of KwaDukuza,
In the large homestead of Ndaba
I stood on the fence and saluted,
I saluted until sunset
When the king's attendant appeared.

He advised me to wait.
A scent entered my nose,
The light shined in my dark mind.
Beautiful Mkabayi came to me.
She looked at me up and down;
I saw the gatekeeper opening the gate.

I entered with my tongue tied,
I sat beside you Dukuza
I was unable to praise like the ancestors.
Sadness and pain I did not feel.
I stretched and I imagined myself being a king;
I slept and dreamed of another day.

I am outside the gates of KwaDukuza.
I looked for Mkabayi but I did not see her;
I looked at the gates and I saw them;
I saw them closed and Dukuza had died.
The tongue filled my mouth.
When I tried to speak I became mute.
Yet I was stealing the power of the praise poets.

Today I cannot keep quiet, although

Where I sleep at the Middle-of-Night
I am waken by Mkabayi saying to me:
"Wake up, you of Mancinza!
You were not born to sleep.
Wake up and praise the stones of the spears!
Here is the burden that I put on you."

(B. W. Vilakazi)

UGQOZI (COURAGE)

Emasangweni akwaDukuza,
Emzin'omkhulu kaNdaba,
Ngem'othangweni ngakhuleka,
Ngakhuleka laze layoshona.
Kwaqhamuka insila yenkosi,

Yangiyal'ukuba ngilinde.
Kwangen'emakhalen'am' iphunga,
Kwakhany'engqondweni yam'efiphele.
Kwafika kim'uMkabayi emuhle, Mkabayi
Wangithatha phansi wangiphonsa phezulu.
Ngabon'umlindi-masango evula,

Ngangena ngishwaben' ulimi,
Ngahlala ngaphakathi kwakho Dukuza.
Angikwazang'ukubonga njengobabamkhulu,
Ukudabuka nezinhlungu angikuzwanga.
Ngenaba ngazicabanga ngiyiNkosi;
Ngalala, ngaphupha ngeny'imini

Ngingaphandle kwamasango kaDukuza.
Ngamfun'uMkabayi ngangambona;
Ngawabuk'amasango ngawabona;
Ngawabon'evaliwe noDukuz'esefile.
Lwagcwal'umlom'ulimi lwami;
Ngathi ngiyakhuluma ngayisimungulu,
Kanti sengintshontsh'amandl'ezimbongi.
Namhla kangikwa'ukuthula noma
Lapho ngilele ngikwesikaBhadakazi,

74

Ngivuswa nguMkabayi ethi kimi:
"Vuka wena kaMancinza!
Kawuzalelwanga ukulal'ubuthongo.
Vuk'ubong'indaba yemikhonto!
Nank' umthwal'engakwethwesa wona.

(B.W. Vilakazi)
[Translated by Gabi Mkhize]

OH! THIS OLD MAN!

It is dignified, your hair!
It tells the roads of years,
It tells the journey of your age,
It revives the grief and jealousy.
I long for it to rake away my loneliness.

It has wisdom, your head!
As I set the walking stick I feel
Its depth, I don't stump the ground.
And you, you left quietly since you didn't know me.
As for me, it was difficult to approach you
Since I didn't know you, but I love you.

In your tears I see there
Goes the sign of the Zulu Nation.
Today the decorated earrings
You have taken them off and thrown them down;
You don't even know where they were left,
And the returned homes where they fell off.

In your eyes I read grief.
Even the tobacco spoon you smoke with
I see that it is taking away the tears
From your watery eyes.
Your mind is no longer here,
And your eyes are looking into the distance.
Far away at the shields of King Shaka,
Down the river pools of KwaDukuza,
There where the water is calm

The heads of elders and their households
They are also grey like you underground.

As you stare, I see
You speak to the elders of the Zulu Nation.
Tell me briefly about the day when I am going to write down
What is heard, what is spoken, and what is seen
In the land of the grayed and the ancestors.
I am looking forward to hear and understand.
Even when you don't respond to me, old man,
It is dignified, your hair;
I love it, it revives jealousy.

(B. W. Vilakazi)

WO, LELI KHEHLA! (OH! THIS OLD MAN)

Zinesithunzi izinwele zakho!
Zibik'imigwaqo yeminyaka,
Ziland'inkambo yobudala,
Zingivus'umunyu nomona.
Ngiyazifisa, zingisus'isizungu.
Linenzulu lelo khanda lakho!
Ngibe ngiyafak'ubhoko ngizwa
Ukujula kwalo, ngingagquli phansi.
Naw' ulokhu wathula ungangazi,
Nami kulukhun'ukukusukela
Ngingakwazi, kodwa ngiyakuthanda.

Endlebeni yakho ngibona lapho
Kwahamba khona uphawu lukaZulu.
Namhl'iziqhaza zokuhloba
Uzikhiphile wazilahla phansi;
Awazi nalapho zasala khona,
Namanxiwa lapho zawa khona.

Emehlwen'akho ngifund'usizi.
Nentshengul'obhema ngayo
Ngiyibon'ikukhiphis' unyembezi
Emehwlen'akho achiphizayo.
Umqondo wakho kawusekho lapha,
Namehl'akho abuka kude.

Kukude ezihlangwini zawoShaka
Phansi ezizibeni zikaDukuza,
Lapho amanzi ezonzobele khona

78

Ngamakhand'amadoda nemizi yawo:
Nawo asengwevu njengawe phansi.

Njengob'ugqolozele nje, ngiyabona
Ukhuluma nezingengelezi zikaZulu.
Chathazel'min'engizobhal phansi
Okuzwayo nokukhulunywayo nokubonwayo
Ezweni lezimpunga nelawokhokho.
Ngilangazel'ukuzwa nokuqonda.
Nom'ungangiphenduli nsizw'endala,
Zinesithunzi izinwele zakho,
Ngiyazithanda, zingivus' umona.

(B.W. Vilakazi)
[Translated by Gabi Mkhize]

TELL ME WHITE MAN

Oh, tell me white man!
Why did you bring me here?
As I entered my knees became heavy;
As I thought the head became confused.
I saw darkness at noon,
The sun turned into the moon.

Oh, tell me white man!
Where am I going to enter in these walls?
The forefathers died, they say.
I should lie down under the grass at Guqa
Where I am surrounded by smoke and dust,
Eating boiled dried hard maize softened with sour milk.

Oh, tell me white man!
Who should I say I would be?
My skin betrays me,
My tongue is good.
Even though others say it degrades me,
I am bewitched by it and I need to be cured.

Oh, tell me white man!
I am utterly lost, where am I going?
The walls of the houses are high,
They go deep down into the ground,
They reach the clouds in the sky.
The Mbozas of KwaNondwengu
They did not see such a thing!

Oh, tell me white man!
What is all this I see?
The pillars are like the forefathers!
When I look at them
I hear the doves up in the sky
Rolling like the lumps of the bulls.

When I see all this
Today I truly believe
I am lost, I will marry.
The nation of Sobantu
Tightens for me the carriage head ring,
We say: "Carry the load and always pass on regards."

(B. W. Vilakazi – Amal' eZulu)

WO, NGITSHELE MNTANOMLUNGU!
(Tell me Whiteman)

Wo, ngitshele mntanomLungu!
Ungiletheleni lapha?
Ngingen' amadol' angisinde,
Ngicabang' ikhanda lizule
Ngibona kuhlw' emini,
Ilanga liphenduk' inyanga.

Wo, ngitshele mntanomLungu!
Ngizongenaphi kulezi zindonga?
Obabamkhulu bathi sebefa
Angolala phansi kotshani kwaGuqa,
Lapho ngihuqwa yintuthu nomule,
Ngidl' izinkobe ngithambise ngomlaza.

Wo, ngitshele mntanomLungu!
Ngothi ngiphi bengiphi nginje?
Isikhumba sami siyangiceba,
Ulimi lwami lona luhle
Nom' abanye bethi luyangehlisa.
Ngibulelwe ngalo ngiding' ukwelashwa.

Wo, ngitshele mntanomLungu!
Ngilahleke nje ngangiyaphi?
Izindonga zezindlu zinde,
Zishona phans' emhlabathini,
Zikhotha' amafu phezulu.
AmaMboza kwaNodwengu
Akazange akubone lokhu!

Wo, ngitshele mntanomLungu!
Yini yonke len' engiyibonayo?
Izinsika zingangobabamkhulu!
Ngithi lapho ngizibheka
Ngizw' amajuba kwelenyoni
Ekhonyis' okwawomalunda.

Lapho ngibona konke lokhu,
Namhla ngikholwa ngempela
Ngilahlekile, ngizogana.
Isizwe sikaSobantu
Singibophel' inkatha yenkangala,
Sithi : "Thwala, usikhonzele njalo."

(B.W. Vilakazi- Amal' eZulu)
[Translated by Gabi Mkhize]

Mgungundlovana; Greytown

One of Shaka's homesteads
Mgungundlovu: Pietermaritzburg

Khahlamba Mountains: Drakensburg Mountains
Langalibalele: John Langalibalele Dube, the founder of the African
National Congress (ANC)

83

Afterword

Mazisi Raymond Fakazi Mngoni Kunene 1930-2006 and Benedict Wallet Mbabatha Vilakazi 1906-1947

Lupenga Mphande

Mazisi Kunene helped establish the tradition of literature in the African languages, not only in his theorizing but also in his practice that span five decades. His creative work was greatly inspired by his Zulu heritage, his commitment to the liberation struggle, his deep belief in, and commitment to, an African renaissance, and his deep appreciation of a literary aesthetics based on the African oral tradition. Kunene believed that to mount a genuine promotion of African literature, the African intellectuals and cultural activists must first commit themselves to the promotion and purposeful deployment of African languages. Only then, he argued, could the Africa intellectuals be in total control of Africa's foundations and the construction of her true literary canon. In this regard Kunene wrote all his poetry in isiZulu, his native tongue, continuing a commitment to the promotion and development of Africa's indigenous languages initiated by earlier writers like Samuel Edward Krune Mqhayi (1875-1945), and Rolfes Robert Reginald Dhlomo (1901-71). Samuel Mqhayi was a prolific writer, renown as a traditional bard and as a modern creative writer, and his Itya lama-wele (The lawsuit of the Twins (1914), which articulated the continued relevance of African culture in the face of European intrusion, became a major inspiration to African writers. R.R.R. Dhlomo, who had written the first novel in English by a South African black writer, An African Tragedy (1928), emulated John Dube and wrote all his subsequent work entirely in isiZulu, producing a series of historical novels about the leaders who had presided over the state of the

Zulu nation.

Thus the writing of African literature(s) in the African languages, rather than in the imperial and hegemonic European languages, was a historical project undertaken by a generation of intellectuals in South Africa as part of a modernization process, and also as a cultural front in their fight against European oppression. The African intelligentsia, within the historical parameters defined by their specific circumstance, recognized the efficacy and agency of culture in their struggle to be heard, and the dialectical unity of agency, structure, and practice in the formulation of a modern African identity.

Therefore, from the very beginning the new generation of African intellectuals in South Africa regarded culture as a pivotal front in their struggle for political liberation, and believed that the creation of a new African consciousness necessitated the creation and organization of their creative work within nationalistic foundations that embraced their literary and cultural history. It is thus impossible to treat Mazisi Kunene and Benedict Vilakazi in isolation, but as part of a movement, with all the political implications that that term encompasses.

Benedict Wallet Vilakazi (1906-47) is generally regarded as the father of modern Zulu poetry, and a pioneer in the study of Zulu language. He was also a reputed essayist and wrote widely for Ilanga lase Natal and other newspapers, which established him as a significant intellectual voice within South Africa. Benedict Vilakazi was born on January 6, 1906 at Groutville, Natal, and died at a relatively young age of 41 on October 26, 1947 in Johannesburg. He was a poet, novelist, and educator who devoted his life to teaching and the study of Zulu language and literature. Vilakazi was intellectually shaped by his stint at Ilanga lase Natal, and the John Langalibalele Dube's Omhlange Institute where he taught for some time. He earned his Bachelor of Arts degree in 1934 from the University of

South Africa and began publishing critical articles and poetry in various journals. Vilakazi earned his M.A. from the University of Witwatersrand in 1938, and in 1948, with Clement Doke, published the Zulu-English Dictionary, which contributed greatly to the broadening of literary intellectual discourse in South Africa. His linguistic and literary works should be viewed within the context of the multiplicity of African languages in South Africa that were garnered up and utilized to facilitate the construction of a unified singular national literature and a new philosophical and nationalistic consciousness. Benedict Wallet Vilakazi's writings, therefore, had great implications on the debates on the identity of African literature and its relation to national culture.

Initially, Vilakazi experimented with the classical English Romantic poetic form, but abandoned it to create a unique genre of poetic style that incorporates the European rhyme and stanza poetic structure into the oral literary form called izibongo, a traditional Nguni praise poetry blank verse form that produces a vivid, dramatic impression, and which many writers who came after him adopted. Izibongo is an oral literary form of expression that evokes a sense of movements and gestures, vivid situations and attitudes, emotions and feelings, colors, presence and absence of sound (i.e., silence), etc. (Mphande, 1993). His first novel was published in 1933, Nje nempela (Really and Truly), becoming one of the earliest Zulu works in a modern literary setting. His first volume of poems, Inkondlo kaZulu (The Zulu Song), came out in 1934, which was followed by two other novels: Noma Nini (No Matter How Long) in 1935, and uDingiswayo ka Jobe (Dingiswayo, Son of Jobe) in1939. Amal'Ezulu (New Horizons), which came out in 1945, was his last volume of poems. Vilakazi's poetry became increasingly agitating and political in the course of his life, dramatizing concern for loss of blood and land suffered by African peoples in South Africa. His novels explored daily Zulu life, and Nje nempela and uDingiswayo ka Jobe were woven around the story of a traditionally polygamous household.

Vilakazi also produced critical works on the Zulu and Xhosa languages: his MA thesis was on "Some Aspects of Zulu Literature" (1942), and his doctoral dissertation, The Oral and Written Literature in Nguni (1946), was a comparative study of Xhosa literature and Zulu literature. In his dissertation Vilakazi pays homage to the Xhosa intellectual Mqhayi to whom he felt particularly indebted. However, Vilakazi examination and analysis of Xhosa and Zulu literary forms are not undertaken to the same rigorous depth as Kunene was to do later in his MA thesis on Zulu literary lineages, An Analytical Survey of Zulu Poetry (1958). On their publication, Vilakazi's poetry and novels were well received, and have remained popular with readers of African literature to this day.

The closeness of Vilakazi's village at Groutville to King Shaka's legendary headquarters at kwaDukuza provided Vilakazi from early childhood with a geographical and historical proximity to the rich references of Zulu identity that occur in his literary works again and again. For example, in a poem entitled "Courage" Vilakazi states:

At gates of kwaDukuza
In the large household of Ndaba,
I stood on the fence and saluted...
Beautiful Mkhabayi came...saying to me
"Wake up, you of Mancinza!"
Wake up and praise the stones of the spears!
Here is the burden that I put on you.
(Courage)

In describing his deep love for the place of his birth, Vilakazi employs the full range of his native tongue, isiZulu, while at the same time also expressing a deep philosophical and emotional side of that experience. Linking land, ancestral spirits, and poetic duty, Vilakazi often stated that his poetic inspiration came from his ancestral spirits, usually couched in the form of a calling, even as a burdensome duty, which he must carry. He said hiis muse usually came to him in his sleep.

Vilakazi was also preoccupied with the theme of alienation and the corrosive effect of city life on unsuspecting, rustic rural folks who migrate to urban centers for employment or other modern glitters. No doubt this was instilled in him by his missionary education. The poem "kwaDedangendlala," for example, depicts alienation from a specific physical location in a strange or foreign land by describing with great nostalgia the geographical features of Durban that the poet was more familiar with: its trees, cliffs, mountains, ocean, etc., against the alienating effects of his new location in Johannesburg. However, in his poetry there is no description of people and their lives and histories – a fact Kunene criticized as 'Romantic'.

In many ways the work of Benedict Wallet Vilakazi, along with the publication of Nyembezi's 1960 A Review of Zulu Literature, and the Sharpeville massacre, marked the end of the rather boardroom type of intellectualism embraced by earlier generation of writers, ushering in a new generation of intellectuals and cultural activists, and a new re-aligning of the political and cultural fronts on the South African stage. In this regard, Mazisi Kunene was fascinated by R.R.R Dhlomo's and Benedict Vilakazi's deployment of Africa's cultural past to build a glorious future, and particularly their appropriation of the Zulu kings to construct a vision of a united front among the ranks of African peoples in the face of foreign aggression. Thus, in his writing Kunene utilized the agency of myth and cultural self-determination found in the saga of King Shaka, particularly the way he brought together the various ethnic groups of southeastern Africa to create a new nation, a nation militarily able to stand on its own feet. Kunene realized that, since liberation means the achievement of freedom and attainment of principles that affect people's daily lives, if there was to be a cultural reawakening in Africa, in general, and South Africa in particular, the way forward had to be through an articulated cultural self-determination. In this endeavor Kunene turned to Vilakazi as his mentor, as he later confesses that "As the Zulu literary tradition had been devalued, I started writing without models, until I discovered Vilakazi's poetry" (1958). Kunene once wished that his poetry would one day appear alongside that of Vilakazi, and this anthology is, in many ways, a fulfillment of that wish and a humble addition to his legacy.

In Vilakazi, Mazisi Kunene found a great inspiration, both in Vilakazi's 1946 doctoral dissertation, The Oral and Written Literature in Nguni, and the historical novels and philosophical poems. He was also inspired by Vilakazi's belief in the utility of African languages in the construction of African identity, as he had once declared "I have an unshaken belief in the possibilities of Bantu languages and their literature, provided the Bantu writers themselves can learn to love their languages and use them as vehicles for thought, feeling and will" (Vilakazi 1939). Vilakazi thus became a spiritual guide to Kunene on the latter's poetic journey to the exploration of African cultural ethos. Kunene acknowledged this in a poem dedicated to Vilakazi "A meeting with Vilakazi, the great Zulu poet," by declaring /before the foreigners came, before they planted their own emblems/I came to the arena and you held my hand/Together we danced the boast-dance of our forefathers/.

However, the tragedy of the Sharpeville massacre made Kunene realize that the ideals of artistic purity espoused by Vilakazi and the older generation of writers had to be re-configured into a political paradigm that would more adequately enable the construction of a program of action to transformed those artistic ideals into the political reality of a people's dream for a better life. Kunene firmly believed that only through a committed deployment of African aesthetics and literary sensibilities could African literature be able to serve its destiny as a critical player in the political, psychological and cultural liberation of Africa and its Diasporas. In Kunene's view, art cannot be separated from politics because, as Mbulelo Mzamane puts it, doing so only serves the interest of the oppressor who invests in such a separation in order to maintain the status quo of unchallenged dominance (Mbulelo 2006: 1). Mazisi Kunene accomplished the task of combining the articulation of an ideal and realization of that dream in a manner few can emulate. He devoted himself to retelling the African story in a way that empowered the people and restored them to their dignified place in the world.

Kunene was born in Durban and grew up in Amahlongwa on the south coast of KwaZulu-Natal. He started writing poetry at a very young age, publishing his works in newspapers and magazine, and in 1956 his poetry collection, Idlozi Elingantethelelo, won that Bantu Literary Competition. He obtained his B.A and M.A. degrees from the University of KwaZulu-Natal, with his master's thesis on Zulu poetry. He taught briefly at the national University of Lesotho before migrating to the School of Oriental and African Studies at the University of London in 1959 for his doctorate. However, the 1960 Sharpeville massacre forced him to abandon his studies in response to the call to duty by the African National Congress (ANC), and he joined forces with Oliver Tambo in intensifying the anti-apartheid campaign, rising to the rank of African National Congress chief representative to London in 1962. Perhaps because of his use of culture as a weapon, his contribution to the liberation struggle has been downplayed, as readily acknowledged by the South African critic and fiction writer, Mbulelo Mzamane (2006:1).

For a long time the measure of Kunene's literary contribution was based on his seminar MA thesis: An Analytical Survey of Zulu Poetry: Both Traditional and Modern (1958), and his two masterful epics, Emperor Shaka The Great (1979) and Anthem of the Decades (1981. The two epics, which are considered as his greatest literary achievements, have no parallels in African literary history, and have been described by K.I. Goodwin as "two most ambitious poems to come out of modern Africa" (Goodwin, 1982:174). Both epics analyze the African philosophy of life as a process of the continual interrogation of the essence and manifestation of African cosmology. Kunene presents African cosmology as foundational in explicating the rationale behind the creation of mankind and the formulation of human social organization. The Zulu believe that a human being is comprised of the body (umzimba) and the spirit (idlozi). During one's life these form a unity, and the spirit expresses itself through character and moral rectitude, but on death the body perishes and the spirit survives. While character and moral weight also survive as spirit, it is only those of exemplary behavior during the life cycle that becomes operative as ancestral-spirits upon death. This status is usually reserved for those who exhibit powerful character or moral force, such as chiefs, clan heads, diviners/healers, military commanders, etc. In Zulu cosmology, therefore, physical life form begins at birth and ends with death, but this physical life form is simply a small chunk in an ongoing process of life that starts as far back as one can remember one's ancestors, and continues almost infinitely in the confident belief that one's sons and daughters will beget sons and daughters who will continue to beget sons and daughters.

Kunene was concerned with the trajectory of colonialism on the African cultural landscape and the resultant rapture in the cosmological epistemology of African life and its effect on the African psyche. It is this underlying concern that forms the genesis of Kunene's constant and urgent appeal to the ancestors or departed spirits to intercede in guarding the African heritage against the whims of foreign forces. He projects the past and the African social values and philosophies that have been handed down from generation to generation as a trusted source for his creative inspiration. Kunene also looked on his writing as a calling, mediated through spiritual intervention: "you are actually inhabited by the spirits on your shoulders and they tell you what to do, what to say" (Kunene, 1993). He felt that the traumatic rupture of African traditions brought about by the colonial intervention necessitated a strong and evocative expository epistemology if Africa was ever going to be re-integrated to its past. He was particularly concerned with the Christian missionary distortion of African history, such as the story of Shaka, the legendary king who founded the Zulu nation in the early nineteenth century, but who was constantly presented as a bloodthirsty despot with no regard for human life. Like R.R.R. Dhlomo and Benedict Vilakazi before him, Kunene felt a unique closeness to the Zulu people, and was deeply attached to their cultural traditions and values and constantly drew on Zulu history, culture and religion as iconographical cultural weapons in the struggle for national liberation.

Kunene set out his literary goal as the retelling of African history in a way that would liberate it from colonial distortions and make it relevant, authentic, and convincing to his audience. Because of his deep conviction in the political function of literature, he dexterously expanded the focus of his poetry to include universal political concerns, the pan-African struggle, social values and serious aesthetic and philosophical issues. Kunene's re-telling of the African story utilized the Zulu oral tradition of izibongo, a poetic form that has a militaristic orientation that afforded him an appropriate platform to agitate for the transposition of the continent's political and intellectual cultures. As a consequence, Nguni's military past, particularly that of Shaka, became such a fascination for him and many South African intellectuals.

In Kunene's creative work, the ancestors are alive in memory as long as their names are remembered, and with Zulu clan izithakazelo (clan praises) still a feature of Zulu life, ancestors may be remembered in this manner for many generations back. The ancestral-spirits can be contacted through dreams, vision, omens, and thanksgiving ceremonies, and also through the mediums and diviners. The ancestors dwell in the mountains, and walk the earth in the moonlight, as Kunene narrates in one of his epics:

After the night has covered the earth
Rouse us from the nightmare of forgetfulness
So that we may narrate their tales
You will see them, the forefathers, by the brightness of the moon.
You will see their great processions as they enter the mountain!!
Eternally their anthems emerge
How then can we be silent before the rising sun?
How wonderful! We can sing the sacred songs of our forefathers!
By our ancient epics we are made beautiful.
(Emperor Shaka the Great, 1979: 1-2)

The references in the lines above to physical features, such as the earth, moon, mountains, sun, etc., are very symbolic and reflective of Zulu cosmology. The ancestors, according to Kunene, dwell in the sacred mountains, and from there, during the full moon, they come to inspect their off springs and guarantee their sustenance and welfare. According to Zulu mythology, in the beginning were two great spirits, one male and one female(s). The male spirit, Mvelingqangi, was austere, fierce, virile, and given to striding through the upper region of space trailing thunder, and the female spirit, Nomkhubulwane, was calmer and more accessible, though both of them could only be contacted by adults through ancestral spirits. Nomkhubulwane is believed to live near bodies of water, exuding mist. She is symbolized by the rainbow, and associated with light, rain, and fertility. In Kunene' poetry, there is frequent references to Nomkhubulwane, and to water as a powerful symbol in the Zulu belief system, constantly reminding his audience of the efficacy of water as a purifying force.

While Vilakazi dwelt largely on the physical geography of his homeland, Kunene delves in the intricate lives of the characters of the histories. For example, Kunene pays tribute to Nandi, Shaka's long-suffering mother in a poem aptly titled "Nandi of Bhebhe:" / You mother, you have walked a long way/ You were not scared with your children/ Please protect our daughters/ They are the main hope of our land/. This poem, written in the vein of Anthem of the Decades: A Zulu Epic (1981), projects women as important citizens in the nation: /They are the main hope of our land/, in other words, without them our nation has no future. In Kunene's poetry, the women are endowed with vision: /They see things at the depth/ They, who don't display their worthiness with muscles/ ... They will mould a big calabash/ So as to quench the thirst of all African nations/. Thus, although women are powerful, they are not ostentatious with their endowment, and definitely do not have the propensity to display their power by flexing their muscle in violence, destruction, and warfare that seem to preoccupy men. Women, the poem says, have a "broad back," that is why they can bear humanity, so that the next generation can inherit wisdom contained in the "big calabash." Kunene presents this as the natural process in human existence. Thus in this poem Kunene upsets the patriarchal structure of Zulu society, and shows great respect for women. He refers to Nandi as the national mother who has stored wisdom "to quench the thirst of all African nations," and thus elevates the position of all women in Africa.

Kunene has a total disdain for European colonists, dismissing them as ungrateful to African hospitality When Europeans went around the world in search of a place to live, he says, Africans welcomes them and gave them land on which to start a new existence – land being so important to African life and existence. But in the end the Europeans turned on them with force of arms and colonized them. Although these people pretended to be people of "substance," most of them were of shady character: ex-convicts, poor, or sickly and ill educated, and yet they ended up amassing great personal wealth by exploiting the Africans and the continent's resources – people like John Cecil Rhodes in Southern Africa and King Leopold of Belgium in the Congo being good examples of the types of Europeans Kunene seem to have in mind.

Kunene also vehemently rejected the colonial system of assimilation, which aimed at turning Africans into "Europeans" by forcing them to abandon their indigenous culture and adapt that of their European colonizer. He dismissed such people as treacherous, as is evident in the following poem:

They have abandoned you, your loved ones
They have run away because you are a disgrace
They have rejected you even in the ears of the nations
Preferring to praise those moving towards assimilation
Speaking in languages that you don't know
So that you do not understand ...
I will plead with them in a soft language
Until they see, until they become enlightened
Until they praise you together with us in ceremonies
(Africa during times of tribulations)

Here again, Kunene appeals to the African ancestors to intercede and enlighten those who have gone astray, and thus restore the fragmented continental community back to its wholesome state

95

where all its citizens can once more partake in the festivals that would enable the community to heal and be back together again. Time and again in his creative writing Mazisi Kunene returns to this theme of the ancestors and Zulu cosmology.

In conclusion, Kunene's legacy on African literature is the consciousness he raised that, to claim its name and fulfill its historical mission, such a literature will have to preoccupy itself with African literature in the African languages. His greatest contribution to African literature and production of knowledge was not only his broadening the boundaries of literary theory in general, but also his tireless and uncompromising crusade in bringing about the birthing and efflorescence of a distinctive breed of African literature crafted from the mother tongue when many of his African contemporaries, such as Chinua Achebe, Wole Soyinka, Ezekiel Mphahlele, Nuruddin Farah, etc., had abandoned their African mother tongues in their artistic practice. In his artistic work, Kunene also de-mystified orality and demonstrated that oral forms are what people speak in their daily lives, and not some sacred breed accessed only by missionaries and anthropological researchers. Kunene's work has also brought about a resurgence of oral research and literary application – on radio, television, political rallies, trade union meetings, and print media – the creative spirit has been unchained, and Kunene has helped elevate praise poetry to respectable level of artistic excellence. Los Angeles Times (September 19, 2006) reported that the ANC distributed Kunene's epic, Emperor Shaka the Great, to its guerillas fighters to inspire them in their fight against the racist apartheid regime.

REFERENCES

Goodwin, K.L. Understanding African poetry: A Study of ten poets, Heinemann 1982, 204 pages.

Benedict wallet Vilakazi, 1939. "African Drama and Poetry," South African Outlook, July 1, 1939,

Mazisi Kunene (1958) An Analytical Survey of Zulu Poetry, M. A. thesis, Durban: University of Natal.

____*Zulu Poems,* Holmes & Meier, 1970

____*Anthem of the Decades:* A Zulu Epic, Heinemann,1981

____*The Ancestors and the Sacred Mountain,* 1982

____*Isibusiso Sikamhawu, Via Afrika,* 1994

____*Indida Yamancasakazi,* 1995

____*Amalokotho Kanomkhubulwane,* 1996

____*Umzwilili wama-Afrika,* Kagiso, 1996

____*Igudu lika Somcabeko,* Van Schaik, 1997

____*Emperor Shaka the Great: A Zulu Epic,* Heinemann, 1979

____*Echoes from the Mountain. New and Selected Poems by Mazisi Kunene,* Okoro, Dike (Ed.) Malthouse Press, 2007

Lupenga Mphande. "Ngoni Praise Poetry and the Nguni Diaspora," in Research in African Literatures vol. 24. No. 4 (Winter 1993: 99-122)

Mbulelo Mzamane (2006. "Mazisi Kunene – imbongi yesizwe," Umafrika, August 25-31, 2006: 1.

B. W. Vilakazi (1942) "Some Aspects of Zulu Literature", *African Studies* 1, 4: 270-274.

_____Dhlomo H.I.E. 1952 Dr. Vilakazi. Drum. Vol 2(7)

_____Doke, C.M. & Vilakazi, B.W. 1953 Zulu-English Dictionary. Witwatersrand University Press, Johannesburg.

Benedict Wallet Vilakazi, 1935 Inkondlo KaZulu. Witswatersrand University Press, Johannesburg

_____1945 *Amal' ezulu.* Witswatersrand University Press, Johannesburg

Works

_____1935. *Inkondlo kaZulu* (poetry), Witwatersrand University Press (Johannesburg).

_____ Noma nini (novel),

_____*Yacindezelwa Emshinini Wasemhlathuzane* (Mariannhill, Natal), 1935.

_____*UDingiswayo kaJobe* (novel), Sheldon Press (London), 1939.

_____*Nje nempela* (novel), Mariannhill Mission Press (Mariannhill, Natal), 1944.

_____*Amal'eZulu* (poetry), Witwatersrand University Press, 1945.

Printed in the United States
By Bookmasters